Security Culture

In 15 years I have read hundreds of security books. Seldom have I read a book with such ambition and scope, impeccable sources, and grasp of what's possible and practical – and what's not – in the business of security management. Any serious security managers wanting to make things happen in their workplaces should open this book.

Mark Rowe, Editor, Professional Security Magazine

Walton combines her academic and theoretical expertise with rich and, almost certainly, unique experience of delivering successful security culture programmes under very challenging circumstances. She offers a precious insight into the world of personnel security and the human factor, and, in doing so, provides a priceless menu of highly practical tips and advice. This is a must-read for anyone serious about security.

Stephen Cooper OBE, former Head of Security,
Olympic Delivery Authority

One of the least understood but most important skills of business management is that of people security. This book demonstrates that there is no point building a digital or physical fortress if staff don't understand the value of security. The author is a respected expert who has not only helped devise security culture programmes, but has also put it into practice in high-profile environments. An essential read for senior executive teams, human resources managers and security teams.

Chris Phillips, Former Head of the UK's National Counter
Terrorism Security Office (NaCTSO); currently the Director of
International Protect and Prepare Security Office (IPPSO)

Security Culture

A How-to Guide for Improving
Security Culture and Dealing with
People Risk in Your Organisation

HILARY WALTON

Routledge
Taylor & Francis Group

LONDON AND NEW YORK

First published in paperback 2024

First published 2015 by Gower Publishing

Published 2016 by Routledge
4 Park Square, Milton Park, Abingdon, Oxon OX14 4RN

and by Routledge
605 Third Avenue, New York, NY 10158

Routledge is an imprint of the Taylor & Francis Group, an informa business

British Library Cataloguing in Publication Data
A catalogue record for this book is available from the British Library

Library of Congress Cataloging-in-Publication Data
Walton, Hilary.
  Security culture: a how-to guide for improving security culture and dealing with people risk in your organisation / by Hilary Walton.
    pages cm
  Includes bibliographical references and index.
  ISBN 978-1-4094-6562-1 (hardback : alk. paper) -- ISBN 978-1-4094-6563-8 (ebook) -- ISBN 978-1-4094-6564-5 (epub)
   1. Business enterprises--Security measures. 2. Corporations--Security measures. 3. Business enterprises--Security measures--Case studies. 4. Corporations--Security measures--Case studies. I. Title.
  HD61.5.W353 2015
  658.4′7--dc23

                                                                                      2014046474

ISBN: 978-1-4094-6562-1 (hbk)
ISBN: 978-1-03-283751-2 (pbk)
ISBN: 978-1-315-60809-9 (ebk)

DOI: 10.4324/9781315608099

Contents

List of Figures

List of Tables

About the Author

Hilary Walton's knowledge base for this book comes from using psychology, risk management and security in business environments. It is based on culture change and organisational development research and theory. It also pulls knowledge from talent management, behaviour change and psychological theories of motivation.

How this theory is evoked in practice is based on working with organisations who wanted to improve their security cultures, across the United Kingdom, Europe and in New Zealand in all sectors, both public and private. The knowledge base is grounded on the author's examples of what organisations have previously done, and the identification of what has been most and least successful.

Hilary is a Chartered and HPC-registered senior Organisational Psychologist and currently works for Airways, New Zealand's air navigation service provider. As their Resilience and Continuity Manager she provides advice to ensure that critical business processes across the organisation are sufficiently resilient to continue operating effectively. Her responsibilities include leadership and oversight of security, change management, business continuity planning, software assurance and safety change processes.

In the United Kingdom she worked for the Olympic Delivery Authority (ODA). This is the organisation that was responsible for developing and building the new venues and infrastructure for the London Olympic and Paralympic Games and their use after 2012. The role she held was Information Security Manager, and she was responsible for the entire Information Security Programme for the ODA, which included leading and embedding security in the culture of the organisation and its contractors.

In her role as ODA Information Security manager Hilary had culture change, privacy and data protection responsibilities in this high-profile organisation. She was involved in the development and maintenance of mutually beneficial working relationships with key UK government stakeholders to identify and mitigate credible external and internal threats;

foster positive and supportive engagement with delivery partners to ensure third-party compliance with ISO-based minimum information security compliance requirements; and provided focus for an effective security training and awareness programme in what was a dynamic, rapidly evolving organisation.

Hilary formerly led projects for a UK government security authority before working for the Olympics, during which she was responsible for briefing stakeholders and organisations nationally and internationally on building a security culture. She also advised on the implementation and interpretation of a security culture tool and delivered change management and action planning workshops to help organisations improve their security culture.

As an Organisational Psychologist Hilary has consulting experience in both the United Kingdom and Australasia. She has worked within both private and public organisational settings, ranging from the Royal New Zealand Air Force through to large government clients and telecoms organisations.

She has been responsible for the design and implementation of people-related business solutions, including those around organisational culture, assessment and performance improvement. She is a commercially astute client and project manager, and has led and facilitated senior stakeholders at a strategic level to effect change.

Acknowledgements

I would like to acknowledge the following people for their kindness and support in making this book possible:

Howard Nichols, Hannah Badland and the excellent team at Gower Publishing for offering their valuable insights and reviews of the pages you're about to read.

My father, Dr Robert Blackmore, who also took the time to review this book and taught me that you can do anything if you work hard and put yourself forward.

My husband, friend and partner Thomas Walton, who gave me the freedom and love required to reach for my dreams. And my children, William and Henry, for supporting their busy mum.

Chapter 1

Introduction

The purpose of this chapter is to:

- Introduce security culture and people risk concepts.

- Discuss the purpose of this book and who it is for.

- Explain how to use this book to improve security culture and reduce the risk that people pose to the business.

So what is this security culture book about? Why it is new and different and why is this area important? Why is there a growing need for information about security culture and people risk management? Here we lay down who this book is for, the purpose of the book and how to use it to improve security culture and deal with people risk in the organisation.

What Is This Book About?

Every business has a unique internal organisational culture that affects how it operates. How an organisation behaves in terms of its style and approach to security is its security culture. Organisational culture pervades every part of an organisation and impacts security. Even with good technical tools and security processes, an organisation is still vulnerable if the general attitude towards security is poor. People risk is the risk associated with people in the organisation compromising security (as opposed to technology risk, which can be caused by things like not having up-to-date antivirus software).

This book is a guide to improving employee attitude, behaviour and compliance in relation to security. It is a how-to guide that helps deal with and improve security culture and reduce people risk in organisations. Failure to give security culture and people risk in organisations the attention they deserve can lead to:

- loss of intellectual property (IP);

- compromised security systems;

- damage to the brand and reputation of the CEO and Board members;

- in the UK, potentially heavy fines by the Information Commissioner's Office (ICO) for data loss;

- major incidents that can threaten the survival of the organisation; and

- minor incidents that can be expensive and time-consuming to resolve.

This book will help security, human resources (HR) and management personnel understand security culture and the risk that people pose to organisations. It will also identify the benefits of leveraging these. It will show how to develop and implement a security culture and people risk reduction strategy and awareness programme that provides measurable results. Based on the author's unique work portfolio, in-depth interviews and research, this book combines proven security culture strategies with ground truth and practical implementation experience to help achieve:

- senior management buy-in;

- greater employee compliance with security procedures;

- reduced unintentional security or privacy breaches;

- increased reporting of security or privacy breaches and employee behaviours of concern;

- reduced ability to manipulate employees or make them less vulnerable to social engineering; and

- reduced vulnerability of insider threat.

It will also help:

- organisations be less vulnerable by deterring high-risk people from joining them;

- improve employee attitudes to security, to view it as an important business-as-usual function; and

- advise on metrics to measure the impact of security culture activities.

These are major and difficult security issues which can have severe and substantial impacts on an organisation. They are difficult to deal with as they extend beyond the security group in traditional terms, and delve into organisational values and norms, management practice and organisational communication.

There is little integrated and structured information on how to embed security in the culture of an organisation. This book draws all the best ideas together and provides an intervention toolkit to pick and choose from when designing a security culture programme.

This book also adds new information from actual organisations which have attempted to develop a security culture across sectors and in private and public settings. It is a vehicle to combine those ideas so that organisations can pick the gems for themselves, those parts that suit their particular context, environment and objectives. It is a method and ideas factory. What is good practice? What is bad? How do I get objective feedback on the bad, which I probably already know about but can't prove? How do I effect long-lasting change in security attitudes and culture? Which are the most effective measures to get more bang for my buck? Are some measures more effective than others? If so, what are they? Currently there is little research and consolidated information about these areas, so this book helps collate this new information in one place. It draws on work within a leading UK government authority on security and advice given to organisations both in the UK and internationally.

Technical security consultancies often attempt to tackle 'people' and 'culture' issues in organisations through awareness alone. This book seeks to move beyond 'security consulting' in the typical IT, physical and awareness sense, and builds upon constructs such as behaviour change and motivational theories. This is where it can add value as it is based on psychological and motivational theory and is written by an organisational psychologist who specialises in this area – and who also happens to be a risk management and security professional with practical experience. The blending of psychology with risk and security is where this book's unique positioning originates. Designed for daily use in an ever-changing world, *Security Culture* covers everything today's security, management and HR professional needs to know.

What Is the Need for This Book? The Rationale

All groups in an organisation need to be able to influence employee behaviour, none more so than senior managers and security personnel. The cost of not doing so is considerable, in the form of security breaches, privacy leaks and damaged reputation. Indeed, there are countless examples of such devastating security or privacy breaches: confidential information found on the street because it was carelessly thrown in a bin; files containing sensitive documents left in a public place; or personal information emailed to the wrong person. The consequences of these scenarios can be severe, and while policies may exist prohibiting these actions by employees, there are no technical or process controls to prevent them occurring (other than physically checking every sheet of paper or message that leaves a building).

Organisations need to do things differently from in the past, and this will involve utilising different skills and methods. It used to be enough to get line managers to deliver security messages to their direct reports and check that these requests were followed. Now, the security team needs to inspire and influence the business towards developing a security mindset. The aim is to have security done as a matter of course; for staff to want to provide feedback about how to continually improve security. This requires managers at all levels to be motivators and communicators and for staff to self-manage and also manage each other's behaviour in relation to security. Managers and employees also need to think of themselves as part of the security team, by proactively identifying potential issues and reporting behaviours of concern, not to mention breaches within the organisation.

But how do we encourage employees to develop and maintain a security-conscious attitude? How do we get employees to behave in the right way? As security professionals, we tell people over and over what they should do in relation to security, but the messages still do not seem to get through. How do we get people to comply with policies and procedures? These are questions consistently asked by security managers and HR professionals as they grapple with the culture and people aspects of their organisations.

This book will help answer these questions. It will use case studies to illustrate good practice and provide resources and interventions which can be applied easily. These issues are timely because security is a growing issue: in part due to recent global terrorist activities that increase national threat levels and risks to organisational and personal safety; but also due to the increased attention organisations and governments are paying to privacy issues and cyber threats. As such, security is an ongoing and escalating issue that organisations are struggling with as they strive to reduce risks as much as possible, and still stay in business.

It is not enough that organisations have good physical and IT security procedures in place to maintain the integrity of the system. If the people in the organisation don't think about security as they go about their work – and don't consider how they can protect the organisation's information, people and assets – then technical controls will not be enough.

So why do organisations need help on this topic at this time? Security culture as a topic is in its infancy. A related field, safety culture, has research and information whose development dates back as far as the Chernobyl disaster in 1986 and the Piper Alpha oil-platform explosion in 1988. As a result, safety culture has become mainstream and has improved business operations. It is likely that security culture improvements will yield the same benefits, but security culture is nowhere near as closely monitored, managed and prioritised by organisation management and executive boards.

While the contents of this book are not a silver bullet to cure a weak security culture and improve people risk management, it is a toolkit of successful interventions to be applied within the unique context of each organisation. It provides a resource for managers to use for advice and ideas on establishing and maintaining optimal security behavioural norms within their organisations. Currently, organisations are attempting to develop these mechanisms in their own way – with unmeasured success.

What Organisational Problems Can This Book Help Solve? What Is It Designed to Accomplish?

This book will help clarify the problem of poor security culture and also assist in gaining buy-in to security as an enabling business function, motivating and influencing employees to follow security procedures and embedding security attitudes throughout the business. Security, and how to instil a security culture, needs to be treated as seriously as health and safety issues.

These 'culture' and 'people' aspects are common areas to be hesitant about. For example, a security manager might find it easy to see how advice about other security disciplines (physical and IT) fit within the usual job responsibilities and duties: security culture, however, is much harder because it is about people and their behaviour. Inevitably, human resources issues will surface, and HR will need to be involved – as will senior management and other employees such as line managers or even the executive board. For example, if it was recommended that an organisation include security in the appraisal process in order to embed behaviour, then this would have to be endorsed from the top, and accepted by HR and line managers trained in how to correctly rate employees on their security objectives.

This book will be a guide to anyone seeking to identify and understand security issues more in terms of behaviour, as well as giving them the confidence to modify existing security practices in organisations at a strategic level. Its aim is to help security professionals influence and motivate employees to want to change their security behaviours, and to change employee attitudes and views of security through motivational theories. It will help people influence employees to want to comply with policy and procedures, and also help them see why it is important to do so – whether for personal reasons because it affects them and their role – but also to see how it fits the goals of the organisation, whether profit, public reputation, quality or safety.

It will be useful to the HR professionals, the security group's essential ally, for ensuring that organisational policies are correctly presented, documented, communicated and enforced. It should also lead to important conversations between HR and IT about matters such as the monitoring and review of staff internet usage and email accounts; mutual difficulties with audits; and IT's internal access to sensitive HR data.

Security Culture will also be helpful to line managers in their role of influencing the training, learning and development of their employees. It is the line managers who bring organisational policies to life and act as change agents, choosing to focus the attention of employees in varying ways.

Summary

Applying the techniques in this book will enable an organisation to introduce or enhance a security culture which will help make security messages stick; get people to comply with policies and procedures; reduce security complacency; get senior management on board; and change employee attitudes to security – to view it as an important business-as-usual function.

The book does this by providing strategies to implement security procedures; illustrating examples through case studies of poor and optimal security practices; existing as a source of inspiration and offering food for thought; and providing a best-practice model by which to manage security culture.

Chapter 2

What Is Security Culture and People Risk? Why Are They Important?

The purpose of this chapter is to:

- Provide a definition of security culture and people risk.

- Outline how the nature of security has changed.

- Discuss the current state of security and what the future holds.

- Ascertain through key questions how secure an organisation is.

- Identify the characteristics of strong and weak security cultures, and why it all matters.

- Ascertain why some organisations have a poor security culture.

This chapter looks at what is meant by the terms 'security culture' and 'people risk' and their effect on organisations. It explains why an organisation's culture and people have an impact on its security. It describes how the nature of security has changed, the reality of where we are now and where we are predicted to go in the future. It also looks at why, although most security professionals agree that people are an organisation's weakest link, they continue to ignore this important area of security – or at best pay it lip service through half-hearted security awareness programmes. In particular, it describes some of the challenges security professionals face in dealing with security culture and people risk, and identifies the skills required to do so. It asks the reader to consider how secure their organisation really is by examining some key questions and areas of their business. It then discusses some characteristics of organisations with strong and weak security-oriented cultures, and with low and high people risk. Finally, the chapter outlines the importance and benefits of security culture and people risk, and why people have so much trouble influencing it or tend to avoid dealing with it.

Security Relies on People to Behave in the Right Way

Let us say that an organisation has in place a range of 'security' measures to safeguard whatever it needs to protect. The organisation might have secure premises or IT infrastructure; controlled access to systems or sites; and operational policies and procedures to govern the way things are done. But security still relies on people to behave in the right way.

An organisation's culture has implications for its security. Even with good technical tools and physical security processes, an organisation is still vulnerable if the general attitude towards security is poor. For example, if there is a general lack of adherence to basic security policies or good practice by employees, coupled with managers failing to notice or address poor security behaviours, then the chances of negative outcomes due to a security breach are increased. Examples of poor behaviours include:

- security cupboards not being closed or locked;

- laptops not secured or locked away when not in use;

- passwords being shared;

- writing passwords down and keeping them in easy-to-find places;

- employees not logging out of terminals or allowing others to use logged-on terminals;

- employees discussing sensitive organisational information in places where they can be overheard;

- not challenging people who are not wearing security passes or, worse, holding the security door open for them so they can enter the building;

- transferring sensitive information on unencrypted memory sticks;

- plugging untrusted or unknown memory sticks into computers;

- reading sensitive information in public places like buses or planes; and

- sensitive material being left on desks or in meeting rooms.

This section explores what can be done about the 'people' and 'culture' elements of organisations, groups or sites to strengthen their security defences against human factors.

What Is Security Culture?

Building a security culture within an organisation is about motivating employees to respect common values and standards regarding security, whether inside or outside the workplace. A security culture can be defined as the values, attitudes and behaviours that an organisation wishes to adopt toward security. The Centre for the Protection of National Infrastructure (CPNI) in the UK describes security culture as:

> The awareness of security amongst staff – their vigilance when conducting everyday routines, for example – is an essential layer of an organisation's protection and staff training, regular drills and internal communications play an important part. But, the manner in which a business reinforces its words is through its actions. If an organisation wants its employees to act appropriately then it must provide an environment that sets an example. For example, if staff are required to keep paperwork securely locked away but they are not provided with sufficient storage (or broken locks are never repaired) they may question the management's commitment to security. But security culture is about more than facilities and procedures, it is also about creating an open, trusted environment that is focused and proactive about reducing risk for everyone's benefit. (CPNI 2013)

As depicted in Figure 2.1, it is useful to think about security culture as an organisation's shared values about what is important. This also includes employees' beliefs about how things work in the organisation. How values and beliefs interact and impact on organisational systems produces behavioural norms. It is these norms that result in the staff behaviour we want to ensure is appropriate for the organisation to ensure it is well protected. So the term 'security culture' captures the values, attitudes and behaviours that impact on the security of an organisation – whether the security of assets, information or people.

Figure 2.1   How security culture is produced

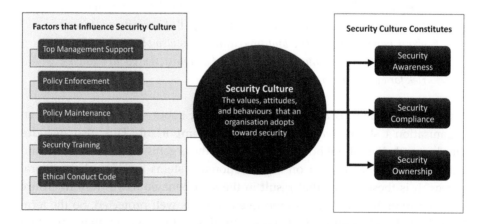

**Figure 2.2   The Alnatheer model of security culture (2012).
Reproduced by permission, Mohammed A. Alnatheer**

Mohammed Alnatheer (2012) looked at 13 security culture models and tools to identify their common components. He found that security culture consists of three factors: awareness, compliance and ownership. This is important because it illustrates that security culture is about more than just security awareness. It is not enough to just make people aware of security; security compliance and ownership need to be influenced as well. He also identified the factors that influence security culture as top-level commitment, policy enforcement, policy maintenance, security training and the understanding of ethical obligations. Figure 2.2 illustrates how these factors interact (see Chapter 4 for more on these issues).

By defining its security culture, an organisation takes steps to promote general understanding and compliance in those who have access to its information and physical assets. Having a defined security culture also allows the organisation to benchmark its approach with others in the public or private sector through surveys and other tools.

Security culture can be changed or shaped by a number of factors. This is done primarily through visible events, management commitment, actions and rewards. It is rarely changed through policy or wishful thinking.

What Is People Risk?

'Risk' is a very commonly used word with a meaning that continues to evolve. The definition of risk in the first international standard on risk management is 'the effect of uncertainty on objectives' (Standards Australia/Standards New Zealand 2009). This definition makes it clear that the fundamental aspect of understanding risk is understanding the effect of an uncertain event on objectives.

'People risk' is the effect that uncertainty linked to an organisation's personnel places on the achievement of its business objectives. The sorts of activities that organisations would undertake to reduce people risk include:

- people risk assessments to identify which roles are critical to the business;

- pre-employment screening and vetting;

- ongoing review of people security; and

- secure contracting practices.

Most security professionals agree that people are a business's weakest link, but this area is still not given the attention it deserves. Business leaders figure that security and privacy breaches will not happen to them; they mistakenly think that they do not have a problem with this; or because they are not aware of the negative consequences of a breach, security is given a low priority and receives little or no budget.

We all know that attackers look for vulnerable areas; they will focus on the weakest links. For example, they do not target online banking directly. Instead, they attack the bank's customers, using phishing techniques to trick them into revealing their credentials. But few businesses think that they could be the target of an attack.

We all know that there are often simple things we can do to reduce the likelihood of data loss and privacy breaches through scenarios such as placing work laptops unsecured under restaurant/cafe tables, or leaving them behind; or, worse, having them stolen. Fraudulent or criminal activity in business is often the result of an organisation giving its people too much freedom or unmonitored access to valuable systems or materials. However, businesses think these kinds of thing cannot be avoided and that 'mistakes' just happen, when in reality people could have been deterred, and these people risks avoided.

People risk security measures help organisations manage the risk of employees or contractors making mistakes or exploiting their legitimate access to premises, information and personnel for unauthorised purposes. Although many organisations regard people risk as an issue resolved during the recruitment process, it is a discipline that needs to be maintained throughout the employment cycle through appraisals, communication programmes, incentive schemes and even management attitudes and relationships. It should also include a formal process for managing staff leaving the business. When consistently applied, people risk measures not only reduce operational vulnerabilities; they can also help build a hugely beneficial security culture at every level of an organisation.

How Has the Nature of Security Changed? Where Are We Now and Where Are We Going?

The security landscape is constantly changing. In 2009 David Lacey argued that what we were asking people to do in relation to security was different from before. He thought that in relation to security we were asking employees to *do more* than what they are told; that we were increasingly expecting them to be *proactively aware* of potential problems and areas for improvement in the organisation, and to be *personally committed* to business goals – whether they be security, safety, quality and (I think it is appropriate to add) profitability – in their day-to-day work. He was right.

This equates to people needing a different knowledge set, and means that employees need to know enough about security policies and issues to be able to converse meaningfully about their impact.

THE REALITY OF HOW THINGS ARE NOW

In this day and age, privacy breaches and cyber security attacks are abundant. Back in 2009, Lacey wrote about a breach of customer confidentiality being one of the most damaging security risks to organisations. The current proliferation of high-profile breaches locally and globally has served to cement that position. Examples include the 2013 Adobe breach when more than 150 million user IDs with hashed passwords were stolen, including those of at least 38 million active users; and the former National Security Agency (NSA) contractor Edward Snowden's leaks about the extent of the US intelligence community's internet surveillance. However, not all data breaches are conducted by highly sophisticated hackers or due to government negligence. Sometimes serious breaches happen because of low-tech carelessness, as described in the case studies (see Chapter 8). For example, in October 2013 more than 729,000 patients were put in jeopardy when two unencrypted laptops were stolen from California-based Alhambra Hospital Medical Center (AHMC) hospitals. Private information – including patients' names, social security numbers and diagnostic and procedure codes – was compromised, affecting six major health institutions overall. Data leakage is a priority for any business process that handles personal data or confidential business information.

It is relatively common knowledge that anything we put on the internet, whether emails or files uploaded and sent through the cloud, should be considered accessible by others. Internet traffic is being intercepted and used by others, for example, criminals, hackers and governments in their war against terror. It can be assumed that we are being eavesdropped on, albeit most likely only the metadata rather than individual emails; but still, when we use the web we leave clear tracks for others to follow.

That said, it is still possible to be secure if we want to, but often we do not bother because secure methods or systems are not as convenient as insecure ones. For example, secure email such as PGP has been around for a number of years now. With this product, messages are encrypted and sent in the usual way; however, both sender and receiver must have the same software for it to work. Or, at the simplest level, organisations could use encrypted USB devices (flash drives) to store information in transit so that if lost (and who has not had a USB drive slip out of their pocket or bag, or just left it behind) there is little or no impact of an embarrassing data leak.

WHERE IS SECURITY HEADED IN THE FUTURE?

In the future, it is likely that less will be spent on defences just at the boundary of IT networks. Instead, organisations will acknowledge that they will be attacked because they are connected to the internet. It is not likely to be personal; it is because cyber criminals' software search the internet for open doors and vulnerabilities. It is also recognised that employees will do things on business networks that they should not, such as uploading/downloading information and, by accident, malware. It is not a question of whether it will happen to your organisation, but of when.

As a consequence, organisations will spend more on monitoring their networks, and will hire experts to do it for them. They will be looking for cyber threats as well as unusual behaviour by employees or others. There will be a monitoring service (in-house or, more likely, an outsourced 24/7 managed service) watching the organisation's network with their hands by a 'red phone' to summon the IT security group when required. For example, if a file behaves suspiciously and looks to be multiplying or trying to raise its permission levels, it will be quarantined, investigated and remediated. Or if an employee uploads, downloads or emails a file over a particular size (a potential data exfiltration incident), IT security will be alerted and will be able to follow up with the employee to see what they uploaded and why. This is an acknowledgement that we cannot stop attacks; there are too many vectors into and out of the organisation, and it is not possible to lock them all down (and still stay in business). The focus will be on identifying attacks when they happen and minimising their effect and impact on the organisation. Cyber incident insurance will become commonplace to cover some of the great costs when such incidents do happen.

Another currently weak area which is predicted to grow in the future is people risk (hence the need for this book). Organisations need to have single accountable ownership and oversight of people risk to ensure that all functions with responsibility for people risk report to a senior, accountable owner. In the future, organisations will take a holistic approach to people security, drawing on such information as IT logs and HR performance appraisals and grievance processes. It is also likely that people risk will be managed like any other corporate risk, but with an important balance of information rights of employees who are subject to workplace monitoring and the security of personal data held by organisations.

Finally, it is predicted that the integrity of business and personal data, ensuring it is not tampered with, will be increasingly important – particularly data that threatens the integrity of an organisation's intellectual assets, as their value is increasing with the information age (Lacey 2009). Integrity breaches rarely happen at present, but when they do their impact is severe. It can be very damaging to the perceived value of a database and the reputation of the business services that depend on it. Whether changes are unauthorised or through mistakes or bad practice, breaches of integrity are hard to detect and difficult to repair.

Having looked at where security is heading in the future, let us turn our attention to examining how secure you think *your* organisation currently is.

How Effective Is the Security of Your Organisation?

How would you answer this question if asked by the executive board? You might reassure them that there is a security management framework in place. The elements of this might include security policies, standards, processes and procedures; assigned security roles and responsibilities; some reporting and training requirements; and, hopefully, some risk assessment process and methodologies are practised. However, just because a framework exists does not mean it is always practised in reality.

Some additional factors to consider in order to give the board, and yourself, assurance are:

- Is the security team given sufficient resources to do the job well? How competent is the security management team? Do they have the respect of management and staff in general? Are they listened to?

- To what extent does management support the organisation's security policies, objectives and controls? Are security breaches routinely reported up the line, trends monitored and serious incidents investigated? When was the last time senior management specifically referred to security in a staff presentation?

- Do staff understand and (rigorously) follow security policies and standards, even when the boss is away? Do the policies and standards cover all the organisation's security requirements comprehensively, and are they up to date? Do new employees and temporary staff follow the same rules?

- Does anyone reward good security behaviour and performance manage poor security behaviour? Do your users understand the need to choose strong passwords, keep them secret and change them frequently? Does anyone check that staff follow security policies?

These questions relate to people rather than technology. Most organisations assess their technology and site access for security risks. However, in my experience, few organisations spend time evaluating the risk relating to their employees, although, the message is now getting through.

Annual reports typically convey the impression that organisations have implemented effective risk management procedures. But security culture and the management of people risk are often neglected as integral parts of corporate risk management.

Security Culture and Managing People Risk Matter

Why should organisations pay attention to what their security culture looks like and what risk their people pose to their business? This next section discusses the characteristics of and impact these factors have on security and on organisations.

CHARACTERISTICS OF A STRONG SECURITY CULTURE

A strong security culture 'does not guarantee an absence of breaches nor freedom from error. It is not the cause of security, but rather a necessary context in which security can be fostered and accepted' (Ross 2011, p. 18). The fundamental tenet being expressed here is that security requires a supportive culture to be effective. A strong security culture therefore has the following features:

- good communication and awareness of risks;

- clarity around how people should handle their job regarding security/risks;

- personal ownership and senior sponsorship (positive tone at the top);

- organisation-wide accepted guidelines and procedures for security;

- reporting and challenging;

- incentives used to reinforce behaviour; and

- enforced disciplinary procedures.

We now discuss some of these general characteristics (the gold standard if you like) – but of course not all organisations are expected to have the same security culture. Its exact look and feel will depend on the organisation's unique operating environment, which will dictate how strict it needs to be, and of course its culture.

Communication and awareness

Communication and awareness of the security risks an organisation faces are paramount. Once security risks are widely understood they can then be handled reasonably. Therefore, if an organisation is to build a strong security culture, all staff should be required to undertake awareness training and annual refreshers at a level appropriate to their role. The culture, and therefore the required security behaviours, should be the same for staff members, contractors, consultants, temp agency staff and those who work through a third party supplier. It is particularly important that senior leaders model the correct behaviours consistently.

Communication to staff of the rationales for security procedures will be deemed important. Staff should understand why the procedures were written, who they apply to and what the intent was. Discussion of security issues will be encouraged, and there should be opportunities to debate weak areas of defence and suggest improvements. Where possible, staff should be involved in discussing security plans and be given an opportunity to influence the way security is handled. For example, a staff working group might have the chance to review new procedures during the drafting phase.

Staff should have awareness of their roles and responsibilities in relation to security. Effort should be made to clarify how individuals should handle their job regarding security/risks. The organisation should be mindful of the fact that employees are an important part of risk management, and in fact part of the security team.

Personal ownership and senior sponsorship

Security procedures should be regarded as an integral part of the organisation's operations, and all those with access to information and physical assets should treat security measures as a personal responsibility. Wherever possible, organisations should involve staff in helping to develop new procedures to ensure their suitability for work areas and to increase commitment when new ways of working are implemented.

Individuals should have a personal responsibility to understand and follow the organisation's security procedures. Anyone found causing a breach through a deliberate action should be held responsible and possibly disciplined.

Managers should encourage a positive and consistent approach to security. They will be held accountable for security breaches if they are found to stem from a lack of understanding of, or respect for, the organisation's security regime. Discussion about security should be encouraged at performance reviews, and in some roles it will be sensible to set specific objectives.

Senior managers should take every opportunity to demonstrate that they take security compliance seriously and to encourage staff to share their ideas on how the organisation might improve its approach.

Employees should take ownership for their security, and even that of co-workers. Staff should be encouraged to adopt personal working practices which make good security integral to everyday work activities and not an onerous add-on.

Organisation-wide accepted guidelines and procedures for security

Security measures should be kept relatively fixed, as a consistent approach will help avoid confusion. They should be well researched and follow good practice (e.g. concerning standards, government policy, or be suggested by staff who best understand the organisation's way of working). Staff should be expected to comply with agreed policies and processes, but there should always be the capacity for change should these processes adversely affect delivery. All changes should be agreed by the appropriate authorised person.

Reporting and challenging

All security breaches and near misses should be reported, and the act of reporting supported as a normal and accepted aspect of the workplace. Anyone in the organisation should feel able to challenge others who are not complying with good security practices, even if they are more senior; and the senior management team should make efforts to encourage this culture so that individuals feel free to expose problems and risks which can then be addressed.

Incentives used to reinforce behaviour

Staff should be recognised for their ideas for improving security and where they have done a good job with security. They should also receive positive recognition for reporting security concerns (incidents or near misses). For example, where appropriate, this might be through a spot award scheme. Managers can reinforce positive behaviour by regularly praising staff and by giving performance in this area serious attention, for example by praising good work and taking time to give feedback in both formal and informal settings.

Enforced disciplinary procedures

Deliberate, malicious or wilful security breaches must be dealt with consistently and rigorously, according to well-established guidelines. For example, regular desk sweeps could be carried out and a letter sent to anyone found to have left sensitive materials unsecured on their desk or in a cupboard which should have been locked.

IMPACT OF STRONG SECURITY CULTURE VERSUS WEAK SECURITY CULTURE

When an organisation has a weak security culture then it is likely to have the following features:

- *Lower levels of compliance.* A poor security culture will encourage an atmosphere of non-compliance to security operating procedures. For example, where some staff's unspoken attitudes to and beliefs about production and delivery outweigh those relating to security or the shape of the environment, the actions of nearby staff can have a highly contagious effect on security practices. In an office where security cupboards are left open, confidential papers are left out on desks overnight and strangers allowed to roam unchallenged, even the best-behaved staff will quickly give up on security.

- *More likely to have unintentional security breaches* – people not doing what they are supposed to.

- *Less inclined to note/report behaviours of concern, or breaches in general.*

- *Employees easier to manipulate/vulnerable to social engineering.* This is the art of manipulating people into performing unauthorised actions or divulging confidential information, usually for gaining computer access.

- *Terrorists or other criminals are less likely to be deterred.* If an organisation appears to have tight security, wrongdoers are likely to move on to one with weak defences. If they see that the security guard lets anyone in – pass or no pass (poor security culture) – then that organisation is more likely to be a target.

To avoid these pitfalls organisations need to develop and maintain a security culture which leads to the right behaviours for their particular situation. However, the one universally accepted feature of security culture is that its influence should extend to all parts of the organisation. There are at least three ways that a poor or inadequate security culture can undermine an organisation's protection:

1. Climate – personnel are not concerned enough about security. A poor security culture is likely to increase the number of weaknesses in the organisation's defence by staff not doing what they are supposed to do. Breaches are more likely in organisations that are insufficiently concerned with workplace conditions that promote slips, lapses, omissions and mistakes by teams and individuals alike. These include inadequate training, poor communication, bad procedures and problems with design of policies and procedures.

2. Awareness – personnel do not understand enough about the impact of security risks. A less than adequate security culture can adversely undermine an organisation's protection when there is no understanding of the risks or when staff do not see the full

extent of operational risks and how these can lead to long-lasting holes in defences. For example, present and potential problems (latent conditions) from project start-up where security has not been considered from the outset may have been bolted on at the end, when it was too late.

3.   Motivation – personnel do not want to deal with security risks. The final way poor security culture has an impact is when there is unwillingness to proactively identify vulnerabilities or deal with known deficiencies in defences. Defensive gaps will be worked around and allowed to persist, for example, if management neglect or postpone the mitigation of a previously identified defensive weakness – 'the case of the unrocked boat' (Perrin 1992).

If organisations are not sufficiently alarmed to do anything about security risks, then a weak security culture exists that can have pervasive effects that not only open gaps and weaknesses, but also – and most importantly – allow them to remain uncorrected. For example, if breaches are never publicised or reported then nobody knows about them, and so the organisation does not learn from them.

WHY SOME ORGANISATIONS HAVE A POOR SECURITY CULTURE

With unlimited budgets and abundant resources, one is sure that when executive boards are made aware of these issues, they would be dealt with effectively. However, one obvious reason organisations find these issues difficult to face – or, worse, avoid the issue – is because there is an economic reality facing security measures.

It is recognised that no business is just in the business of being secure. They need to manage risks pragmatically by keeping them as low as reasonably practical and still be economically viable. That said, it is now increasingly clear that few organisations can survive a catastrophic organisational breach or terrorist attack. So why do some still have really weak security cultures? There a number of subtle economic factors at work:

- There is a close relationship between the amount of risk taken and profitability. There is little gain without pain, or at least the likelihood of it. To remain competitive, many companies must operate a moderate risk zone with occasional excursions to the high-risk region. For some organisations there is even the blinkered pursuit of commercial advantage; and

- Time or delivery pressures; cost-cutting or cost pressures.

For other organistions it is the indifference to risks. There is no willingness to do something about risks that have been identified. The impact of a poor security culture still remains. Therefore, any work done to improve security culture and people risk needs to be strategic and hit the mark. The tools in the following chapters will help do this.

References

Alnatheer, Mohammed A. 2012. *Understanding and Measuring Information Security Culture in Developing Countries: Case of Saudi Arabia.* PhD thesis. Brisbane: Queensland University of Technology.

CPNI. 2013. *Security Advice: Personnel Security – Security Culture.* July 17. http://www.cpni.gov.uk/advice/Personnel-security1/Security-culture/.

Lacey, David. 2009. *Managing the Human Factor in Information Security: How to Win over Staff and Influence Business Managers.* Chichester: Wiley.

McIlwraith, Angus. 2006. *Information Security and Employee Behaviour: How to Reduce Risk through Employee Education, Training and Awareness.* Aldershot: Gower.

Perrin, C. 1992. British Rail: The case of the unrocked boat. *Workshop on Managing the Technological Risk in Industrial Society,* May 14–16. Bad Homburg, Germany.

Ross, Steven J. 2011. *Creating a Culture of Security.* Rolling Meadows, IL: ISACA.

Standards Australia/Standards New Zealand. 2009. *AS/NZS ISO31000:2009 Risk Management: Principles and Guidelines.* Sydney/Wellington: Standards Australia/Standards.

Chapter 3

Building the Business Case for Security Culture and People Risk Management: Getting Senior Level Buy-in and Commitment

The purpose of this chapter is to:

- Provide a strategy for getting senior level buy-in.

- Outline how to develop a security business case.

- Outline business case features.

- Discuss the real cost of a security breach.

- Help enlist a senior level champion.

This chapter is about one of the most important elements in getting any business strategy or initiative off the ground in an organisation – getting senior level buy-in and commitment. Many research articles and books talk about it as vital, but how exactly is it done in reality? This chapter outlines some techniques and steps for securing the support of the senior staff, including calculating the real financial costs of a security breach and enlisting a champion on the executive team. It also provides sample resources, such as a paper to put to the executive board and a business case.

Nothing happens in organisations without a strategy and plan of action. Without a business case, a strategy or plan will not get the resources or finance it needs. No business case will be accepted without the support and commitment of the senior executive team. Implementing a strong security culture and controlling people risk in an organisation needs ongoing top-level leadership, commitment and support to be truly effective. If this support is not available, it should be found. Failure to do so will mean that any behaviour change programme will have limited success.

One of the things employees in an organisation pay considerable attention to is what the people immediately above them in the business hierarchy pay most attention to. People take their cues from others, particularly those with a power base or authority over them. This is because in organisational settings messages and cultural norms cascade through the levels from top to bottom. For example, if your boss thinks that being on time for work is important, it is likely that you will try to be on time to meet their expectation. If your boss does not mind people coming in late, then you can bet that you and the other direct reports would come to work later. This is called following the herd and it is a powerful motivator and behaviour builder. Mark Earls (2009) wrote about the herd concept in his book about how to change mass behaviour. More about herd behaviour is discussed in Chapter 5 regarding interventions to improve security culture and reduce people risk.

Start with a Draft Strategy

The best place to start the ball rolling is to draft a strategy for managing security culture and associated people risk. Security culture permeates every department in an organisation, and coming up with a strategy can be a complex task. It should form part of the overall business plan and should be aligned and integrated with other existing plans. For example, strategies may also exist for general security, safety, IT, knowledge and information management, human resources (HR) and communications.

I suggest creating a draft strategy first because it can be difficult to get cooperation or input from other groups for a strategy if senior support is not already in place. No one wants to waste time and effort on activities that eventuate to nothing. In addition, to get the support of the whole senior team an 'executive supporter' to 'champion' the cause and work is needed. This champion will need to be convinced and won over with a sound business case, which they will use to lobby and convince the rest of the executive team. So come up with a draft strategy and business case first, based on what is known about the organisation and the risks it is exposed to, so that there is a framework for discussing how security culture and people risk affect the business.

Develop a Business Case

A business case is a document that outlines the reasoning behind a project. It is used to justify why the organisation should agree to the proposal and provide the necessary resources and budget. It should include anything that might affect the project's success or failure, outlining benefits, costs and risks. It is a means to inform and communicate key ideas and the proposed plan of action. It might take the form of a written document or PowerPoint presentation, but it should always be in a form consistent with the organisation's usual approach.

BUSINESS CASE FEATURES

To facilitate acceptance of the business case for implementing a security culture and people risk management strategy address the following.

The proposal's objectives must demonstrate a link or alignment with the organisation's objectives to show immediate relevance with the business direction.

It is useful to illustrate potential consequences of failing to achieve certain objectives and regulatory compliance. It should persuade the senior decision makers to consider its value, risk and relative priority. For example, the UK's Centre for the Protection of National Infrastructure (CPNI) advocates the use of a basic risk assessment. This would include an analysis of risks, their impact and their probability. A simple way to assess the cost effectiveness of a proposed risk is to compare the cost of implementing a control with the cost of not implementing it. If it is assumed that the probability will sit somewhere along the scale of 0–1, then multiplying the cost by the probability gives the weighted risk, which can then be compared to the cost of the control (Centre for the Protection of National Infrastructure/CPNI 2009). That said, the data needed to calculate the probability of and impact from people risk incidents is often subjective and not widely shared, as in confidential business cases for boards. In addition, it can also be because organisations that suffer incidents fear a loss of employee, customer, partner or shareholder confidence if those incidents become public (CPNI 2011). That said, recent research by organisations such as the Ponemon Institute can help justify the real cost of a security breach, as the next section details.

The real dollar cost of a security breach

A good way to discuss security programme effectiveness is by considering the actual cost of a security breach. A common misconception is that the cost of a breach is solely from the loss of productivity due to system unavailability. However, a major survey by the Ponemon Institute (2013) of 1,069 business continuity specialists and 1,247 IT security practitioners (representing 20 industries and 37 countries) showed that a staggering 80 per cent of the cost of a breach is from other factors, broken down as:

- 30 per cent reputation and brand damage costs;

- 22 per cent forensics to determine root causes and technical support to restore systems (IT costs)'

- 20 per cent lost productivity due to downtime or system performance costs;

- 19 per cent lost revenue; and

- 9 per cent compliance and regulatory failure costs.

These figures were shown to apply to breaches due to human error, IT system failures, cyber security or data breach/theft, third-party failures of continuity or IT security, loss from data backup or restore failure and natural or man-made disasters.

A best practice, quick and easy security incident calculator developed by Symantic and the Ponemon Institute works out what the real dollar cost would be for organisations, based on the answers to a few simple questions.[1]

The cost of a breach plays a significant part in justifying and building the business case for spending on security. These costs should be highlighted to management to demonstrate the impact of breaches on organisations.

Here are some more facts about the real cost of IT security breaches. While minor events obviously cost less than substantial events – a minor event lasts only a few minutes (the survey quotes an average 19.7 minutes) as compared to a major event which can last much longer (on average 422.3 minutes) – when you divide the duration of disruption or compromise (minutes) by the total costs, minor events actually cost 65 per cent more per minute than major events.

---

1   Symantic and the Ponemon Institute, <http://www.databreachcalculator.com/>.

The value of these kinds of survey lies in their potential to influence senior management decisions on the overall funding for security risk mitigation. Presenting costs in terms of business impact is crucial to building a business case for investments. Assuming that business costs are greater than the cost of investing in risk mitigation, the business case then becomes one of either preventing losses or increasing revenues – while at the same time protecting one of the organisation's most critical assets: its reputation. The key is to ensure that management understands that security risks affect the organisation's revenues, reputation and brand image (Ponemon Institute 2013).

According to the Ponemon research, the most likely cause of business disruption is human error – the people in the organisation. It is also the most costly. The 2013 survey showed that for IT security breaches or data breaches/ theft, human error was responsible for an average of 31 per cent of risk-related disruptions in 24 months. However, if an organisation had strong security procedures in place prior to the breach, the average cost was reduced to $13 Australian (AUD) per compromised record. In addition, an incident response plan, business continuity management and the appointment of a chief information security officer (CISO) saved the organisation as much as $10, $9 and $3 per compromised record, respectively (Ponemon Institute 2014). Indeed, IBM believes that:

> the number one essential best practice: building a risk-aware culture and management system that begins at the top and is pushed relentlessly down throughout the organisation. This involves identifying sources of risk, setting goals and communicating roles and responsibilities at every level, from senior and middle management to every user of the organisations systems. (Ponemon Institute 2013)

This is even more powerful if you extend the security culture programme to include suppliers and third parties where possible to mitigate breaches by these organisations.

If you are wondering about the chances of your organisation suffering a data breach, research shows that the potential risk to sensitive and confidential organisational information is high. The probability of a material data breach in the next two years involving at least 10,000 records is nearly 18 per cent (Ponemon Institute 2014). So it is not a matter of if a breach will happen, but when.

MORE BUSINESS CASE FEATURES

The business case should also evaluate each option to enable senior executives to determine whether the proposed programme is of value to the business and achievable compared to the relative merits of other options. It should show the proposed options and the reasons for rejecting them. The options should also include the case for not initiating a particular project.

Funding issues are key factors so that these can be quantified and evaluated. The budget breakdown for each option should be included so that comparisons can be made. Common project risk/benefit or financial models should also be included, such as return on investment (ROI), to quantify the programme's benefits and cost. However, ROI may only provide limited utility in matters of culture and security risk, so this should not be the only factor used (CPNI 2011). It is likely that safety and compliance will be the most important factors, as senior management, executives and the board are accountable for these and should therefore invest in these areas, particularly if they want to avoid litigation. This is how to justify the programme's value.

The business case should also define and identify the monitoring and auditing measures that will be included in the programme, to enable it to be measured objectively and the subsequent achievement of its benefits to be found.

It is common for organisations to commission a consultancy to develop the business case on their behalf. This is because consultants may have greater knowledge of the relative likelihood of security and people risk, based on their dealings with other clients and up-to-date industry knowledge. There may also be other reasons a consultancy is used, for example the benefit gained from an objective third party undertaking the work. In any case, the consultancy will need to work closely with the client to ensure that the business case is relevant and tailored to the organisation. It is the business which will understand the priorities, 'pain points' and 'hot buttons' of the executive team.

Appendix A presents a sample proposal for funding for an information security, security culture and people risk management business case which can be used as a guide for commissioning a consultancy. This example gives an idea of the format and possible topics; however, organisations are advised to tailor it to their own requirements.

Find an Executive Champion

An executive champion will be the gateway to the executive team, the board and the organisation's business agenda. They should be briefed regularly on security culture and people risk issues and will be your voice at the executive table and in the boardroom. As the saying goes, 'If you can't be at the table, ensure your messages are.' They are the vehicle for doing so.

So who should be the executive champion for security culture and people risk issues?

> *All organisations have a chief information security officer (CISO), whether or not anyone holds that title or not. It may be the chief information officer (CIO), chief security officer (CSO); chief financial officer (CFO); or, in some cases, chief executive officer (CEO). (ISACA 2011)*

The scope and breadth of this topic, particularly from an information security standpoint, means that the authority and responsibility required will inevitably rest with a senior executive or C-level/suite person (ISACA 2011). This is especially due to legal responsibility and liabilities, but also because of an organisation's growing dependence on information and the growing threats from its own employees and contractors. An organisation's appointment of a single accountable owner helps ensure that security culture and people risk are assessed and mitigated effectively, as other organisational risks.

Since security culture, and people risk in particular, is comparable in importance to other corporate risks, organisations should apply the same supervisory principles in managing people risk. As with other organisational risks, the CPNI (2011) says that, in dealing with people risks, audit committee principles should include, ensuring that:

- the committee is fully informed of the organisation's methods and has approved them;

- the committee regularly reviews people risk and takes an active interest in its status; and

- people risk is the explicit responsibility of a non-executive director to balance the executive discharge of this responsibility.

Now that a champion has been identified, it is important to secure their support. To secure a senior executive's support it is important that they understand the message and the sorts of things to lobby for. A draft strategy gives the platform from which to script the message and business case. A final strategy demands that other groups in the organisation be involved.

Further Develop the Strategy

Developing an effective security culture and people risk strategy requires integration and cooperation with business process owners. For example, if the security culture strategy calls for changes or tweaks to employee induction and screening processes, then the HR team will naturally need to be involved. If executive support has not been gained from the outset or communicated to other groups and teams then lack of action, indifference or defensiveness will stifle or hinder any progress. A good security culture and people risk strategy must be aligned to and support business objectives.

It should be noted that tension often exists between IT and security departments. It is common for the former to face performance pressures, while the latter must obviously deal with security and often safety issues. These different agendas generally fall at opposite ends of the spectrum, and the outcome can put strain on the groups. This can only be rectified by senior management fostering cooperation and arbitrating differences in perspective. Senior management should ensure that they strike an adequate balance between delivery, performance, cost and security (ISACA 2011).

The hallmark of a good security culture and people risk strategy is the effectiveness with which it achieves the desired objective of providing a predictable, defined level of assurance for business processes and an acceptable level of impact from adverse events (ISACA 2011).

Use a Champion to Get the Strategy Approved

The next step is to get the strategy or work programme signed off by the executive team, using the support of the champion. This is usually done by presenting a synopsis to the board, and will require liaising with the champion and the board's secretary/personal assistant (PA) to get the item on the agenda.

Once on the agenda, the aim is both awareness of security and people risks and the impact of a weak security culture – and of course to get the programme supported and secure funding. Appendix B gives a sample presentation to an executive board to secure funding for a security culture and people risk awareness programme. It provides an idea of the format and topics which may be included; however, organisations are advised to develop a tailored version according to their own requirements. ISACA (2011) provides a good list of evidence of executive and senior executive support and commitment that includes:

- clear approval and support for policies in the form of signatures on documents from the CIO or equivalent;

- supporting awareness and training for employees by engaging them in the programme;

- sufficient resources and authority to implement and maintain security activities;

- high-level oversight and control;

- treating security as a critical business issue, fostering a strong security culture and rewarding/praising security behaviours in staff;

- periodically reviewing security effectiveness and risk registers;

- reinforcing security aspects or issues in organisational updates to all staff; and

- setting an example by adhering to the organisation's security policies and practices.

If some or all of this is apparent in your organisation, then you have secured your senior management.

Revisit Executive Team Commitment and Support Later in the Programme

As discussed, it is important for senior management to not only support the programme, but also to walk the walk and talk the talk. Senior management should be seen practising good security culture behaviours and strategies to manage people risk. For example, if the organisation issues security passes/badges but senior management do not wear or display theirs, this sets a bad example. General staff members will question why they should wear passes if the senior management team do not. This weakens the organisation's security culture.

Another important point here is that senior executive support should be obtained not only at the outset, but also reinforced throughout. Failure to do so is at the peril of the programme. Senior management should be reminded of upcoming security events and activities, particularly those affecting them, to ensure support and engagement. They should also review key security risks periodically to ensure that they remain critical business issues. How to determine security culture and people risk is the focus of the next chapter.

References

CPNI. 2011. *Holistic Management of Employee Risk (HoMER)*. London: Centre for the Protection of National Infrastructure.

Earls, M. 2009. *Herd: How to Change Mass Behaviour by Harnessing our True Nature*. Chichester: Wiley.

ISACA. 2011. *Certified Information Security Manager CISM Review Manual 2012*. Rolling Meadows, IL: ISACA (formerly Information Systems Audit and Control Association).

Ponemon Institute. 2013. *Understanding the Economics of IT Risk and Reputation: Implications of the IBM Global Study on the Economic Impact of IT Risk*. White Paper. United States: IBM Corporation.

———. 2014. *2014 Cost of a Data Breach Study: Australia*. Traverse City, MI: Ponemon Institute.

Chapter 4
Assessing Security Culture

The purpose of this chapter is to:

- Outline the benefits of measuring security culture.

- Provide ways to measure security culture.

- Discuss practical considerations of measurement.

- Explore models of security culture.

- Provide a brief outline of security culture assessment tools.

This chapter explores some of the benefits of measuring security culture and people risk. It examines how one might measure them and some of the practical considerations of measurement. It also looks at some existing models of security culture and assessment tools.

The Benefits of Measuring and Improving Security Culture

When considering the assessment of security, often people think about threat assessments, risk assessments, IT network architecture assessments and physical and information security assessments. Rarely are an organisation's security culture and people risk considered, studied or measured.

In order to have an effective security strategy, it is first essential to measure the current state of the organisation's security culture and its people risk. A measured starting point provides the platform for diagnosis of the security issues and plans for improvement. Ongoing measurement enables the organisation to determine whether its security culture is improving. Measurement helps an organisation to not only monitor and manage its security culture and people risk, but also assists with:

- business strategy development;

- business strategy implementation;

- culture change;

- organisational sub-culture identification;

- organisational health checks; and

- diagnosing problems and barriers to strategy implementation.

Measurement of security culture also complements other organisational culture measurements, for example, employee engagement, satisfaction and wellness surveys.

INTEGRATION OF SECURITY CULTURE AND PEOPLE RISK MEASUREMENT WITH OTHER SYSTEMS

Security culture and people risk assessment outcomes build on the foundations of other existing organisational systems, including the most obvious one – security management – but also quality management, health and safety and environmental safety management. In particular, quality management may well be already established in most organisations. The introduction of security culture and people risk measurement can feed into quality management systems as an enhancement of current practices, such as introducing a proactive risk-based approach to security.

Integrating with other organisational systems also has the benefit of reducing duplication of resources and eliminating conflicting objectives. It will improve the collation and analysis of security related data and enhance the recognition of security as important for organisational success.

Some of the key benefits that can be derived from measuring security culture and people risk management in an organisation include:

- identification of security culture and people risk responsibilities;

- a common and comprehensive approach with regard to security management;

- better understanding of risk for defensible decisions;

- documentation of reasons for best practice;

- provision of a visible audit trail;

- reduction in litigation potential;

- avoidance of over-engineering;

- compliance with legislation;

- creativity and innovation in management practice;

- increased level of accountability;

- improved capacity to manage in the face of competing obligations;

- transparency in decision making;

- compatibility with regard to risk practice;

- increase in the likelihood of achieving stated security objectives;

- effective resource allocation;

- fulfilment of 'duty of care' considerations;

- support for a structured approach to planning; and

- improved efficiency of process.

The very act of conducting a survey constitutes an intervention – a signal sent to the organisation about the security culture. People are likely to wonder what is happening, how they can help, and how it will affect their work and their employment. They are likely to look carefully at the outcomes and the process: is this a genuine attempt to listen and make changes or a way to please the regulators (Carroll 2002)?

Practical Considerations and Pre-Planning Before Measuring Culture

When measuring aspects of culture, the process should be approached as a change management project that needs careful thought, pre-planning and resourcing from senior management. Measurement is not enough; it is also important to consider how to communicate and implement the results for meaningful change. In carrying out a measurement project, it is important to consider the following factors.

WHAT IS THE AIM OF MEASURING THE ORGANISATION'S SECURITY CULTURE AND PEOPLE RISK?

Typical aims for a measurement project are to shape the design of a security strategy for the organisation. It can provide a benchmark of organisational culture from which to measure performance that can be used for comparison over time, and so establish whether the organisation is improving. The comparison between groups/departments within the organisation is also possible to ascertain where attention and resources should be focused. It can help prioritise security efforts within the company and diagnose problem areas in the organisation and barriers to change. It is also possible to use the measurement of security culture to build the business case as further justification for increased budget/funding of interventions such as awareness or assurance programmes.

SENIOR MANAGEMENT BUY-IN

The importance of management buy-in cannot be overstated. Management support and participation are very important for success in conducting security culture surveys, as well as for ensuring there will be some follow-through actions. The use of a senior executive champion of the process should assist in obtaining meaningful commitment to changes. If you cannot be at the executive table yourself, then you need to get your messages there via a champion and supporter.

COMMUNICATION WITH STAKEHOLDERS

Communication with key stakeholders including, where appropriate, unions is important throughout the measurement process. Relevant internal stakeholders may include the following.

- Human Resources (HR)/People Group: It is typical for the HR or People teams to coordinate or provide oversight of any surveys occurring in an organisation. This is usually to ensure that surveys are relevant and that employees do not get overburdened with internal survey requests. This helps achieve better response rates and buy-in from employees. The HR group will have their own surveys occurring throughout the year, such as an engagement survey, so there may need to be negotiation for the best placement of the security culture survey around others during the course of the year. Another key tip – engage the HR/People team early to avoid delays, solicit their buy-in and help remove obstacles later down the line.

- Communications team: The communication team is another key stakeholder to speak to and engage early in the process. They tend to be the watchdog for the organisation's brand. The communications team will want to ensure that appropriate branding is placed on the survey. This may be the organisation's brand, or it may be more appropriate to brand with the external company branding of the survey tool used. They will also wish to ensure that the language and messaging surrounding the survey is appropriate to the organisation.

- IT group: Depending on the survey/measurement tool used the IT team may need to be engaged to host the tool on the company's network. For example, it may be possible for the IT team to put the survey on the intranet and/or make use of the company's active directory to track participants. Alternatively, the survey may be provided by an external party or be a software program uploaded and therefore no internal IT group contact required. This can be advantageous if company IT is outsourced and therefore any requests for help come with a fee which may even further stretch a tight security budget. It might be useful to ask the HR group how they host their surveys to get an idea of what has been done before. The right mode of hosting required for the survey will depend on the tool used and should be based on advice from the IT team.

Gaining agreement from stakeholders from the outset will optimise buy-in to the process, getting meaningful results and follow-through actions.

DEVELOPING A PROJECT PLAN

Security culture and people risk measurement as part of a change management process will require project planning for each phase of the roll-out. This
includes seeking senior level agreement to conduct the survey, communicating the
results and implementing any desired change. The measurement process can
take longer than expected. For example it might take a minimum of six weeks
before being ready to launch the survey to employees due to the stakeholder con-
sultation required; hence the importance of early discussions with stakeholders.

ALLOCATING RESOURCES

A survey project typically requires a small number of key people to be
responsible for sending questionnaires to participants and running the
analysis. These need to be trusted individuals who will ensure confidentiality
of individual responses.

IDENTIFYING A REPRESENTATIVE SAMPLE

Getting everyone in the organisation to respond to the survey is the best situation
possible. Realistically, however, a 10 per cent minimum sample from specific
employee groups is enough, with an optimum 20 per cent representation. Ensure
that respondents are randomly selected and that it is possible to link the groups
to the aims of the survey, for example wanting to determine any differences
between groups. When communicating results, the response rate attained will
be a key factor to create buy-in to results. The higher the response rate the more
credibility and validity the results will gain. It is possible to use sample size
calculators found on the internet if you are interested in a scientific approach
to ensure that results reflect the target population as precisely as possible.

PERSONALISING THE DEMOGRAPHIC SECTION

Typically at the start of a survey some brief details are obtained about the
respondent; this is called demographic information. Most surveys have the
ability to enter terminology specific to the organisation to make the results
more meaningful, for example business unit, job level, geographic location.
It might be important to provide guidance on completing the demographic
questions in the covering letter to participants so that they define themselves in
the survey in the way intended. This is particularly relevant nowadays where
people may work from multiple locations. It is also useful to define different job
levels, for example so that people understand what is meant when the survey

states 'senior management' versus 'middle management' or even 'technical management' in the demographics section of the survey.

Take the opportunity to link the security survey to aims specific to the organisation by asking additional questions which are separate from security culture. For example, find out if employees understand and use the organisation's document classification scheme, or whether there are any issues with finding relevant information in security policies.

MAXIMISING RESPONSE RATES

It is important to advertise the survey internally prior to sending out for the most responses possible, for example in meetings, newsletters or via the senior champion. Think about what has worked well with previous organisation questionnaires. Is it possible to time the distribution of the survey to minimise demand on respondents? Is the purpose of the survey clear? Has enough time been provided for staff to complete it? Does the organisation have available a 'completion thermometer' to drive responding? If possible, personally email reminders to all staff to boost the response rate (alternatively, enlist a communications or HR representative to do so).

DEFINING A COMMUNICATIONS STRATEGY

This is key to enabling buy-in from employees for helping to ensure valid responses. Once again, consider what has worked well previously and ensure transparency by stating the survey's aims and timeframes. Think about the options available to get the message across, for example posters in staff rooms, kitchen areas or toilets; screensavers; messages embedded in the quarterly all-staff briefing from the CEO; intranet news articles; company magazines or newsletters; and company conferences.

TELL EMPLOYEES WHAT WILL HAPPEN WITH THE RESULTS

Explain in advance what will happen to the survey results and how they will be made available to the organisation. It is essential to make a commitment to do this or the survey will do more harm than good.

CONSIDER RUNNING A TRIAL SURVEY

Running a trial survey first with a small sample will help eliminate any questions that are unclear and gain confidence in the logistical arrangement.

Models and Assessment Tools

It was discussed in Chapter 1 that security culture as a construct is in its infancy. While it is gaining some momentum and there is agreement that establishing a security culture is necessary for effective security management, there is a general lack of academic research into its empirical measurement. So when models are discussed, it is important to bear in mind how valid a model might be and whether there is good-quality research behind it.

One of the most basic and commonly used ways to gain information about security culture and people risk is a checklist or survey assessment.

CHECKLIST ASSESSMENTS

Checklist assessments are a common form of diagnostic tool. Often they consist of yes/no questions that help people determine whether specific factors are in place or not. Example security checklist items are:

- 'Does the board discuss security at each meeting?' Yes or No.

- 'Have employees been briefed in the last three months on the security threats the organisation faces?' Yes or No.

- 'Do employees understand where to report security breaches to?' Yes or No.

- 'Does the organisation have a strategy in place for developing a security culture?' Yes or No.

The benefits of using a checklist assessment is that it is possible to ascertain what the organisation does or does not have against what others have identified as presumably security best practice. This will gauge the types of things that can be put in place if necessary. It will also help consolidate a vast amount of knowledge and reduce the influence of halo effects or other measurement biases because, in answering yes or no, something either exists or does not.

It is important to evaluate whether a checklist is clear, comprehensive, complete, easy to use, fair and pertinent to the content area. This last point is usually the biggest issue because checklists are a simple diagnostic tool, and so there is often not enough information available to ascertain whether they are based on sound models of security culture and people risk. Checklists do not usually afford any information on priority in order to give corrective actions. It is also unlikely that there will be information to determine which activities will be important to shape the sort of culture the organisation requires. Below is an example of an effective checklist which can be used to measure security culture.

WINS checklist

The World Institute for Nuclear Security (WINS) has produced a security culture checklist. It consists of a number of yes/no questions to ask of the board, executives, facility managers and supervisors and staff. While the context of the checklist is the nuclear industry, the same questions could be used in other industries. The purpose of the checklist is to help establish the overall health of an organisation's security culture. It has also scored the overall responses to help assign a level of maturity to the security culture on a five-point scale ranging from 'Ineffective' to 'World Class'. Level 1 describes organisations that believe security is an unnecessary, expensive burden enforced by national regulators. At the other end of the scale, level 5 describes organisations that believe security is highly important and that all stakeholders in the organisation – from the board to the workforce – have an important role to play in it.

The checklist forms part of a series of International Best Practice Guides (BPGs) on nuclear security culture and can be downloaded from the resources section of the WINS website on becoming a member.[1] Membership to WINS is free and they invite applications from organisations and individuals with accountability for nuclear security *and* who wish to contribute to the goals of WINS – to share and promote the implementation of best security practices. However, applicants do not necessarily need to work in the nuclear industry to be accepted. The website makes it quite clear that effective security for nuclear and radioactive materials often relies on different organisations working together in partnership with clear definitions of accountability and good communications. For those reasons WINS is inclusive and recognises the importance of having members with different accountabilities and experience. Membership is therefore open to policy makers, regulators, responders, facility operators and related occupations in central government, government organisations, research establishments and private companies. A key component of membership is showing how the applicant will share and promote the implementation of best security practices.

---

1 https://www.wins.org.

A step up in terms of sophistication from a simple checklist is the use of a survey. In this case, more information is gained, not just simple yes or no information. Surveys generally ask the respondent to answer the questions along a particular scale or continuum to see how effectively or ineffectively a particular initiative is working in an organisation. The next section will now discuss some existing surveys and questionnaires that can be used to measure security culture and people risk.

SECURITY CULTURE AND PEOPLE RISK MODELS, SURVEYS AND QUESTIONNAIRES

As already mentioned, the measurement of security culture is not straightforward because of the need to measure the concepts of both 'security' and 'culture'. In fact, literature reviews reveal that there are actually some key gaps in current knowledge. For example:

- there is no accepted, practical definition of security culture;

- research into how security culture can be engendered and enhanced is narrowly focused on specific aspects of culture; and

- there is a lack of research relating security culture to organisational performance (Alnatheer 2012).

The above gaps are, however, not surprising given that it has already been established that security culture as a field of study is in its infancy. So where should one start to measure security culture in organisations? The good news is that some authorities have already proposed models of security culture and people risk and have built surveys and questionnaires around those. Three such surveys are outlined here.

WINS Security Culture Survey

The World Institute for Nuclear Security has also produced a Security Culture Survey, in addition to the checklist described above, to help organisations evaluate the views of four key audiences: the board; executive and chief nuclear officers; facilities management and supervisors; and employees. The survey aims to assess the following factors by asking no more than 16 questions (WINS 2011):

1.   The board and executive view – whether they focus regularly, and to the appropriate degree, on security. This involves assessing

whether 'nuclear' security policy has been developed, communicated effectively, expectations made clear, and the degree to which the workforce values security.

2.   Facilities management, supervisors and employees' view – whether they appreciate the kinds of threats they face, understand their security responsibilities, and have consequently adopted good security practices.

3.   Risk view – the threat and potential consequences of a security event are fully recognised throughout the organisation, and whether the risks are managed within the framework used to manage other key business risks.[2]

The second security culture survey and accompanying model to discuss is one the author has intimate knowledge of and has used scores of times with different organisations.

The CPNI's Security Culture Review and Evaluation Tool

The CPNI, the UK's Centre for the Protection of National Infrastructure,[3] first launched SeCuRE, the Security Culture Review and Evaluation Tool, in 2009. This followed extensive research into security culture. Since then the tool has been used by over 60 critical national infrastructure organisations in the UK. It is regularly reviewed and updated accordingly. The third iteration, SeCuRE 3, was released in 2014. It was the first tool to measure security culture specifically. The tool is made up of two questionnaires and an accompanying software package to help with survey data analysis and interpretation. SeCuRE 3 combines information about an organisation's current and target security culture with a measure of its security climate.

To ascertain the current nature and desired aspirations of a company's security culture the tool seeks information from senior stakeholders in the organisation about what approach they believe their organisation should take to manage security (the desired culture) and what approach it currently takes to manage security (the current culture). The output is a gap analysis that visually represents similarities and discrepancies between the current and desired security culture.

---

2   The survey can be accessed via the *WINS Security Culture Best Practice Guide* and downloaded from the WINS website on registration; https://www.wins.org.

3   http://www.cpni.gov.uk.

A survey is also given to all employees to produce a snapshot of the organisation's security climate by asking how they feel about the way security is handled or managed within their organisation. Participants rate their level of agreement with statements regarding security. The tool combines the culture and climate information to give a view of an organisation's performance in relation to its security culture.

The SeCuRE tool model of security culture, security climate and behaviour change

The SeCuRE tool is based around the Competence Assurance Solutions (CAS) Culture Management Model (Johnson 2008) (see Figure 4.1). This model states that culture change management begins with senior management agreeing a clear idea of the type of culture the organisation would like. The

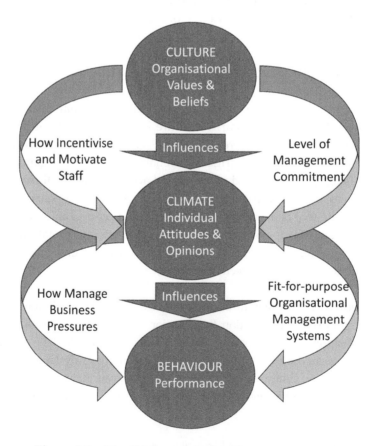

Figure 4.1   The CAS model of culture management.
Reproduced by permission, Competence Assurance Solutions (CAS)

challenge is then to embed the desired culture into the organisation using a mix of motivational techniques (e.g. incentives) and management support (e.g. management commitment), and then enable staff to adjust by putting in place the appropriate systems and resources (e.g. organisational systems and business pressure management) (CPNI 2009).

To build the desired security culture – the shared set of beliefs, values, attitudes and behaviours within an organisation towards security – it is important to influence people's individual attitudes and opinions, the organisational climate. These are influenced by the sorts of incentives an organisation uses – for example feedback, praise, coaching, tangible rewards such as pay and promotion, as well as staff involvement and empowerment. The commitment of management is also a powerful attitude shaper: for example, through the extent to which management visibly supports security issues; and the degree to which an organisation learns lessons from the past, provides support and resources to security activities and engages with its staff on security matters.

Once the security climate is in place then it is possible to see staff performance or behaviour change. Behaviour change is sustained when the organisational management systems are effective and fit for purpose. In addition, if the appropriate change management systems and human resources process are in place, then staff competence and behaviour can be maintained. However, the best systems will not be effective if some elements of the organisation are misaligned. For example, if staff do not feel that their colleagues share the same common attitudes and are adopting the same security practices then behaviour will not be consistently applied. The organisation also needs to support employees' work practices when faced with opposing work demands to ensure goal conflicts are reduced. If an organisation looks after its people well and if the staff trust each other to behave in security-conscious ways, then the right behaviours can be expected to shape and maintain the desired culture.

While the senior manager survey helps define the current and target security culture of the organisation, the employee survey helps identify which of the mechanisms above need improvement in order to build the desired culture.

The next section discusses recent research conducted by Mohammed Alnatheer to discover which factors comprised and influenced security culture so that it could be measured (Alnatheer 2012).

Alnatheer Model of Security Culture and Assessment Tool

Alnatheer looked at 13 security culture models and tools to see what the common components of security culture were. He identified three factors that constitute security culture:

1. **Security awareness** – Employees must be aware of the security policy. In order to create an environment that promotes security culture creation, security awareness must be established (Alnatheer 2012). The lack of security awareness itself has been repeatedly considered as a major problem for ensuring the security of organisations. Security awareness can improve employees' behaviour directly by influencing them to contribute to the establishment and maintenance of a security culture (Alnatheer 2012).

2. **Security compliance** – Security culture can be created if compliance with security policy is achieved (Schlienger and Teufel 2003, 62). 'By compliance with a security policy, organisations are able to decrease the number of security breaches which result from employees' behaviour. Employee's misbehaviour could also influence information security practices which might cause damage and loss to the organisation's assets' (Alnatheer 2012, 136–137).

3. **Security ownership** – 'It is important for staff in any organisation to understand their security roles and responsibilities, in order to enhance their own security performance and thus the organisation's security performance. By understanding their responsibilities and the importance of protecting information security, staff are able to understand what security risks are associated with their actions. This will increase their security awareness levels, which will increase compliance with the security policy of the organisation. For this reason, employee responsibility and ownership of the need to protect information security is an important aspect of creating a security culture. By being responsible and having a sense of ownership, staff behaviour will change with respect to protecting organisational assets, leading to the creation of a security culture' (Alnatheer 2012, 137).

In the same study Alnatheer also outlines the following factors that influence or shape security culture:

- **Top management support and involvement** – Top management need to support and be involved in security. Their commitment and involvement in security is considered one of the *most* important factors for improving or creating security culture and an environment that supports security (D'Arcy and Greene 2009, 127).

- **Policy enforcement** – being able to enforce policy changes attitudes and behaviours. A common way to do this is auditing and monitoring the security policy, practices and procedures. Using an external independent auditor is particularly valuable in helping to achieve enforcement.

- **Policy maintenance** – continually reviewing, updating and improving the security policy, procedures and programme. This could be done through risk assessment and change management; understanding the risks and improving the policy based on risk reduction.

- **Security training and awareness** – being able to communicate the security policy to staff in the organisation in order to influence their behaviour and create a security culture.

- **Ethical conduct policies** – understanding ethical obligations. Ethical conduct policies (e.g. professional conduct, code of conduct, conflict of interest) assist users in understanding and being aware of their security responsibilities and help to reduce risk associated with their security behaviour. This would also help users adhere to the security policy.

Figure 4.2 presents the factors that comprise security culture and the influencing factors as prescribed by Alnatheer (2012).

Based on the outcome of qualitative interviews and synthesised literature review analysis, Alnatheer went on to develop and validate a reliable information security culture measure based on this model (Alnatheer 2012). The research model was statistically tested for validity and reliability with 254 participants representing different industries, types, sizes and roles in Saudi Arabian organisations. While the tool was developed for the Saudi Arabian context, it is applicable to other environments.

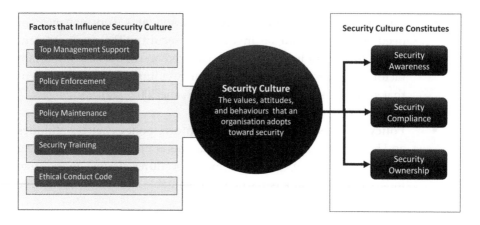

Figure 4.2   The Alnatheer model of security culture (2012).
Reproduced by permission, Mohammed A. Alnatheer

Alnatheer's model is a useful one and we can see some similarities between this and the CPNI's model of security culture, which is promising given that both models claim to measure the same thing. However, while Alnatheer's model has identified some factors that influence security culture, it is not necessarily a causal model that leads from security culture to security behaviours.

The next chapter – the Intervention Toolkit– will consider both the CPNI and the Alnatheer security culture model.

References

Alnatheer, Mohammed A. 2012. *Understanding and Measuring Information Security Culture in Developing Countries: Case of Saudi Arabia*. PhD thesis. Brisbane: Queensland University of Technology.

Carroll, John S. 2002. Conferences and Symposia. *United States Nuclear Regulatory Commission*. Accessed April 20, 2015. https://nrc.gov/public-involve/conference-symposia/ric/past/2002/slides/t6backgr.

CPNI. 2009. *Concept of Use for the Security Culture Review and Evaluation (SeCuRE) Tool*. London: Centre for the Protection of National Infrastructure.

D'Arcy, J. and G. Greene. 2009. The Multifaceted Nature of Security Culture and Its Influence on End User Behavior. *IFIP TC 8 International Workshop on Information Systems Security Research*, May 29–30. Cape Town.

Johnson, Charles E. 2008. Organizational Culture and Effect Sizes. *9th International Conference on Probabilistic Safety Assessment and Management. IAPSAM.* Hong Kong.

——— . 2010. Creating an asset management culture. In *Asset Management: Whole-Life Management of Physical Assets*, ed. C. Lloyd. London: Thomas Telford.

Schlienger, T. and S. Teufel. 2003. Analyzing Information Security Culture: Increased Trust by an Appropriate Information Security Culture. *Paper presented at the DEXA Workshops.*

World Institute for Nuclear Security (WINS). 2011. *Nuclear Security Culture Revision 2.0: A WINS International Best Practice Guide for Your Organisation.* Vienna: WINS.

Chapter 5

How to Improve Security Culture: Intervention Toolkit

The purpose of this chapter is to:

- Outline the overall categories of mechanisms to influence security culture.

- Provide the mechanisms to influence senior management commitment and support.

- Provide the mechanisms to reward and specify incentives for the right security behaviours.

- Provide organisational systems as mechanisms to shape security culture.

- Provide the mechanisms to influence business and organisational pressures.

- Provide the mechanisms to develop a communication and education programme and build security awareness.

- Provide the mechanisms to build security ownership and compliance with security practices.

Now that there is an understanding of what an organisation's security culture and people risk might look like, the focus turns to how to improve them. What can actually be done to get the organisation where it needs to be? This chapter examines the components of security culture and people risk, and introduces interventions. This is the heart of the 'toolkit' from which to pick and choose interventions to target specific weaknesses identified in the organisation. This way, the chosen interventions will better fit a particular organisation, its people and its unique environment. Where possible, interventions are outlined and examples given with 'how-to' guides to adapt and use straight away without going through potentially lengthy design processes, consultancy services or further training. The resources in this chapter include over 250 interventions and/or guides. Appendix C also provides an example of a communications plan.

The saying 'it won't happen overnight, but it will happen' applies to security culture change management. It is true that there is no magic bullet, no quick way to change an organisation's culture. It takes time. The good news is that there are many methods to influence organisational culture.

As an organisational psychologist, information security and risk management specialist this is the part of the process I enjoy the most – picking the interventions to build, shape, develop or maintain a unique organisational culture. The interventions described in this chapter are all linked to psychological theory, motivational theory, and behaviour and culture change. They are also aligned with the security culture models presented in the previous chapter. They will, therefore, describe how it is possible to:

- influence senior management commitment and elicit their support;

- influence the way staff behaviour is reinforced through tangible and intangible incentives;

- plug into existing organisational or human resources (HR) systems;

- manage workplace pressures and conflicts that may hinder or block a particular culture being enabled;

- develop a communication and education programme and build security awareness; and

- build compliance and ownership of security practices.

Overview of Mechanisms to Develop a Security Culture and Reduce People Risk

Figure 5.1 outlines the general category of mechanisms used to shape security culture which have been adapted from the Alnatheer security culture model

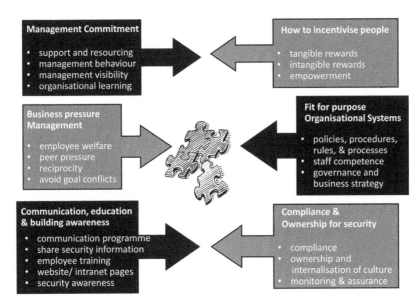

Figure 5.1   Mechanisms to build security culture and reduce people risk

(2012) and the CAS cultural management model (2008). Each mechanism is outlined and associated interventions are suggested to describe how it can be used in practice in business and organisational settings.

Mechanisms to Influence Senior Management Commitment and Support

The greatest influences on individual performance are the expectations of leaders. Security is most effective when managers and supervisors of the organisation continually demonstrate their commitment and support for security through their words and actions.

Managers influence security culture throughout their organisation through their leadership and management practices. With sustained effort, and by employing the incentives and disincentives at their disposal, they establish patterns of behaviour and even alter the physical environment. Senior managers are responsible for defining and revising policies and protection, and operational managers are in charge of initiating practices that comply with these security measures. Through their behaviour, managers demonstrate their commitment to security, and in doing so play an important role in promoting security culture within the organisation.

THE IMPORTANCE OF SUPPORT AND RESOURCING

When the security function is supported by senior management through what it says and does, this sends a strong message to the organisation that it is viewed as a critical business function.

Create management interest

The authority associated with the position of management means that they have the capacity to influence people in the organisation. The management group act as role models, and how they behave impacts the behaviour of staff. If management show a lot of interest in security and routinely follow security policy, then staff are more likely to do so as well. In organisations with a weak security culture, management who are not very interested in security, results in employees not displaying proper security behaviours. This mechanism is a powerful social force that can change staff behaviour if utilised appropriately.

Mechanism	Intervention Activities
Use evidence to provide a burning platform	Consider how to give security a higher status in the organisation, as this will encourage senior management interest.
	Have there been any security breaches in the organisation recently to provide a burning platform?
	Can security breaches in the media or case studies as examples of what could go wrong and what could happen to the organisation be used?
	Have there been any credible surveys or research about security breaches and their impact that could be used as evidence to raise the interest level?
	Check previous audit reports for findings relating to security.
Build systems that promote management interest	Embed security into organisational systems to help keep it at the front of management's mind, for example:
	Report quarterly to the management team on the performance of the security programme. A traffic light system (red, amber, green) could be used to draw attention to security elements that are not performing well.

	Ensure security risks are identified and incorporated into any existing organisation-wide risk programme. Extreme and high risks could be reported to, and tracked by, the board for more visibility. After all, security is a business issue, not just a security group issue. Include security as an agenda item at meetings to prompt people to discuss it. Ask people to identify current or emerging security risks or concerns. Meet management teams or functional groups across the organisation monthly to discuss security matters and identify good and poor security behaviours.
Show how security impacts business achievement – WIFIM (what's in it for me)	Build awareness of how security affects business results amongst management. Tailor messages to WIFIM to ensure they have the most impact on the audience. For example: • When speaking to a sales and marketing team, discuss how poor security or a breach could affect their ability to tender competitively for work or affect a relationship with an existing client. • When speaking to a finance team, draw on how poor security could lead to fraudulent behaviour. • When talking to HR, focus on the confidentiality of staff information. • In discussions with the communication and brand team, messages relating to a breach's effect on the organisation's reputation and negative press from a security incident will help ensure they sit up and listen. • When speaking to operational staff, messages about how critical systems and process could be affected and brought down are key.
Keep material presented to seniors fresh, or risk losing their interest and support	If the material you are presenting at senior level is not kept fresh and not regularly changed, then this group will adapt to it and, after a while, not notice it at all. This phenomenon is called hedonic adaption (Lyubomirsky 2013) which can be harmful to the programme's continued support from the senior team.

Give security importance organisationally

If an organisation is committed to security, it will give ongoing messaging about security to its people. There are various ways that this can be done.

Mechanism	Intervention Activities
Include security in management and team meetings	Include security issues in management and team meetings. Think about how often this happens in the organisation. If not very often, then think about why. Is it a resourcing issue, a time issue or a cultural issue? That is, not how things are done around here. Managers are responsible for setting appropriate standards of behaviour and performance associated with security and for ensuring that expectations as to the application of these standards are well understood. Therefore, these messages are well suited to discussion in team meetings.
Two things staff should understand from managers about security	Managers should foster an effective security culture by ensuring that people understand that (IAEA 2008, 13): • credible threats exist; and • security is essential.

How to secure appropriate resources and funding for security

Does the organisation ensure that security receives an appropriate share of resources and funding? Security programmes should be properly budgeted for and resourced. When they are not, this is a sign of a weak security culture.

Mechanism	Intervention Activities
Build a business case	If budget or resources are a problem for the security programme, then a business case should be developed requesting funding. The risks to the organisation, expressed in financial and other business terms, for not having security in place should be identified.

Find ways to share resources	Identify if the work of other groups in the organisation is aligned with or interrelated with the work of the security group. For example, likely compatriots are HR, the safety office, risk management, quality or assurance teams. Is it possible to team up with any of these groups to share budget or work plans, or get them to promote your security messages and procedures?
Learn from others' mistakes; leverage media articles	Media articles provide a safe mechanism to learn from other organisations' security breaches without the negative impact of experiencing them yourself. Use relevant media articles about security breaches or related issues to support the case for more funding. Often these articles will discuss the cost of the breach, which can be factored into budgeting proposals.

Influence how management behaves and responds to security deviations

As is the case with any breach of an organisational policy, the quicker it can be responded to the better. This is also true when responding to security breaches. For example, delaying an investigation into a security lapse de-emphasises the importance of the event and makes it harder to get staff to amend their security behaviour.

Mechanism	Intervention Activities
Provide managers with security resource information	Provide managers, supervisors and team leaders with the security tools and templates they need to help them fulfil their security responsibilities. These sorts of resources, if easily found and accessible, either in hard-copy information packs (pocket-sized cheat sheets might be useful) or via the organisation's intranet, will save them time and effort. An added benefit is that it will help ensure the correct procedure or policy is followed. The sorts of tools one could imagine here are: checklists or even scripts for what to do in the event of a security breach; forms and templates to fill in when an employee joins, moves or leaves the organisation; and checklists for the return or change of IT, devices and access to systems.
Train managers and publish standards of behaviour	For employees to have positive security behaviours, they need to be aware of what they can and can't do. There are some key organisational documents they should be aware of. These include the various security policies (i.e. IT acceptable use policy, information security policy, physical security policy, personnel security policy and employee code of conduct). These documents indicate the standards of behaviour expected.

Hard copies of this information are often handed out in induction packs, but this can quickly become outdated. A useful vehicle for this sort of compliance training is eLearning modules |

	(computer-based training) which tests the knowledge of the person upon completion of the module and also tracks who has completed training. Annual refreshers should also be conducted. While this sort of training should be run organisationally wide, it is important that managers not only complete the training but also model and manage the right behaviours of staff. Specifically, managers should (IAEA 2008, 31): • lead by example and adhere to policies and procedures; • personally monitor performance in the field by walkthroughs, listening to staff and observing staff at work, and then taking action to correct deficiencies; • demonstrate a sense of urgency to correct significant security weaknesses or vulnerabilities; and • be able to recognise degraded security conditions and take corrective action.

THE IMPORTANCE OF MANAGEMENT BEHAVIOUR

Behaviour is an observable action or statement. Staff are inclined to learn and imitate patterns of behaviour in their group/department; and, once established, these patterns are hard to change. It is important to demonstrate that management deals fairly and justly with security matters. Management behaviour should reflect accountability, professionalism and integrity in dealing with security issues.

Deal with security matters consistently

To reiterate, the principles of procedural fairness should apply when considering security breaches or lapses. Fairness should be enforced so that consistency is maintained, but the action should be proportionate to the intent of the breach. For example, a wilful breach might require harsher disciplinary action than a genuine act of human error. Whatever the case, the same rules should apply no matter the level within the organisation. Inconsistency in disciplining security breaches can undermine the effectiveness of security policy and encourage a weaker security culture.

Mechanism	Intervention Activities
Follow policy and justify deviations	When dealing with security breaches, consider the history of how these have been addressed in the past. Ensure consistency

	and demonstrate this if possible so that the message to staff is clear that seniority does not play a role in how breaches are dealt with.
Apply 'just culture' principles	Consistency in behaviour can be more readily gained when a 'just culture' exists. The goal is to balance accountability with learning. Refer to Sidney Dekker's work for more information.

How to get staff to accept responsibility for security

The security department does not own security; the business should own it. The security group is not accountable for security; they should provide oversight and assurance. The *business* is accountable for security. Therefore, it is important to get staff to accept that they have responsibilities and play a role in the performance of security in the organisation. The saying 'the standard you walk past, is the standard you accept' is as true for security as it is other subjects like safety and quality.

Mechanism	Intervention Activities
Provide security goals or objectives	Security goals or objectives can help teams break down onerous rules and policies into bite-sized chunks: e.g. that all staff secure their laptops away at the end of the day; that all staff collect their printing from the printer after pressing the 'print' button; that all sensitive paper waste is disposed of for confidential shredding in bins provided; that all USB or memory sticks used by staff are encrypted. It may be useful to formulate the five or six most important or essential security rules you want staff to follow, as a way to engender the right *basic* security behaviours. This may help form useful security awareness campaign messaging.
Make good security performance public	Consider ways to publicise the good security performance of different areas of the business. Could the results of random area desk sweeps be made public on a company intranet? If it would not be palatable to publish poor results, could you publish good results? If security behaviours are considered at quarterly performance review, can these group level results be published internally? Could an annual security performance award be made to a team, and can individuals be recognised for good security behaviour? It might be helpful to consider how good security behaviour aligns with organisational values, as this is often a useful mechanism to uncover rewardable behaviour.
Analyse the systems and databases and assign accountable managers to information assets	All systems and databases within an organisation should be identified and assessed to understand the information they hold and how it is used. The assessment should consider what the information is, how it is moved about, the systems that support it and also the locations it is held in by the organisation and individuals (CESG 2009).

	Once these systems are identified, then senior managers should be named as 'business process owners' or 'asset owners' so there is a clear line of responsibility for the security of those assets and the information they hold.
Monitor risk management practices	Monitor how managers manage the risks in their areas (or of their teams) through key performance indicators (KPIs). Do unacceptable risks have action plans or mitigations identified to reduce them? Are those actions being completed promptly? If not, are the risk/action owners being held accountable?

Reduce blame culture

If there is distrust and fear in an organisation, and staff blame each other to avoid being reprimanded or put down, a blame culture exists (Butler 2012). It is necessary to reassure staff that they will not be seen as difficult if they raise security concerns. Otherwise, staff may choose to not bring problems to the attention of management, or those who do may feel that they are viewed as difficult and therefore limiting their career potential.

Mechanism	Intervention Activities
Have a process to raise security concerns	Ensure a process exists for all staff to raise security concerns directly with immediate managers, senior managers and regulatory and other bodies if appropriate.
Encourage staff who raise concerns	Make it clear that staff who raise legitimate security concerns are encouraged and seen as good organisational citizens. A feedback loop is important here to ensure that staff who raise concerns understand what happened, or didn't happen, as a result.
Ensure security/ organisational values and security principles expressed in policy are 'lived'	Ensure security (and organisational) values and the security principles expressed at policy level are 'lived' in an organisation and build a shared purpose. Examples of security principles that are common in policy are: 1) the function of security should create value: 2) security should be an integral part of organisational process; 3) security risk management is embedded in day-to-day decision-making; and 4) security controls are based on risk assessment. When focusing on a shared purpose, this not an expression of the company's enduring essence, but a description of what everyone in the organisation is trying to do – e.g. 'doing what is right and not what is easy in relation to security matters'. It guides efforts at all levels, from top management's business strategy to teams of individuals. Properly understood, a shared purpose is a powerful organising principle (Adler et al. 2011).

Adopt a 'just culture'	Adopt a 'Just Culture' to security concerns. This will enable open and transparent reporting and discussion of concerns that will in turn foster learning for the future. When an error or incident occurs, the question asked should be 'What went wrong?' not 'Who was wrong?' (Butler 2012). The focus should be on improvement, not blame, unless the behaviour was of gross negligence or criminal behaviour

Always be professional

A professional approach to security can mean the difference between a strong and weak security culture. If organisations do not act professionally, consistently and with integrity in security matters, then security can be undermined. If staff see managers acting unprofessionally about security – e.g. senior managers are not wearing ID passes when it is policy for all staff – this impacts the credibility and effectiveness of the whole security system. Managers should serve as positive role models through their attention and adherence to security practices.

Mechanism	Intervention Activities
Investigate unprofessional acts	Managers should not abuse their authority to circumvent security or cover up breaches. If managers do behave unprofessionally or inconsistently a root cause analysis is useful to determine what is really going on in that situation. Is there a particular cause or are there other contributing factors that make that act possible? Is the act malicious or is the intent good, but the process, or system, is contributing to the wrong behaviours identified?
Qualities of professional and inspirational leaders	Being professional in the workplace is important to lead people effectively. Some qualities of professional and inspirational leaders: (Goffee and Jones 2000): • They selectively show their weaknesses. By showing some vulnerability, you reveal your approachability and humanity. • They rely on their intuition and emotional intelligence to gauge the appropriate timing and course of their actions. • They manage employees with 'tough empathy'. This means they are honest and realistic when giving feedback and they genuinely care for their people's welfare. Feedback is delivered with the mindset of helping the other person improve next time.

	• They reveal their differences to capitalise on their strengths and what is unique about them. This can also be called finding your leadership voice.
Lead by example	Ensure that managers lead by example and from the front in terms of their security behaviours. The human brain contains mirror neurons that fire up when we watch someone doing something, be that hitting a tennis ball or disposing of confidential information appropriately (Ramachandran 2012). This is called empathy, and for most it is an automatic response. Staff do not see managers doing something and consciously think they should be doing it too. It is their brain's automatic system, which is much more powerful and influential than telling someone they 'should' do something.
	To support senior leaders to lead by example, they can be taken through a structured process by which the desired behaviours are identified through interviews and/or workshops. They are assessed on how well they demonstrated them and provided coaching. This process will help break down barriers; align behaviour around newly defined core behaviours; and develop language that allows leaders to share their views and critical tensions openly. Executives then emerge from this process more capable and able to lead the transformation of the organisation.
	Also, personal interaction creates trust far more rapidly than phones, emails, letters and so on. So ensure face-to-face interaction where possible.

HOW TO INFLUENCE MANAGEMENT VISIBILITY

To model the way in terms of the right security behaviours, leaders and managers need to be visible to staff so that they can see those positive behaviours.

How to improve management contact with employees

Staff want to see their senior leadership and management, and they should want to have contact with them as well to stay connected. Also, this is a powerful way to influence employees and inspire a shared vision. Face-to-face interaction creates conversation and can help compliance. Managers should be encouraged to visit staff to talk about security. Ideally, managers should participate in security conversations and updates, or even introduce security training sessions more often. This shows they visibly support the security function.

Mechanism	Intervention Activities
Involve senior management	Involving staff in security training or refreshers enables them to talk with staff on a personal level about why security matters. It also shows they care about it and see value from it. This is made even more powerful when managers spend time observing, correcting and reinforcing staff performance in the workplace.
Spoon-feed managers security messages	Managers should make themselves approachable and allow effective two-way communication. It is important to make it easy for managers to discuss security. Providing them with the right messaging via briefing packs is a good way to help ensure they deliver messages to the organisation.
Stress the importance of face-to-face interactions with staff	Whenever possible, encourage managers to deliver security messages face to face and explain the criticality of this medium. Electronic forms of communication such as messages on a company intranet, emails or instant messaging (IM), while efficient, lose impact and can be misinterpreted.

How to improve the reporting of security concerns

It is important to have a well-used reporting mechanism in place. This includes for security breaches as well and near misses. Staff and contractors should also be encouraged to report other security-related concerns or observations of unusual behaviour – 'see something, say something'.

Mechanism	Intervention Activities
Make reporting a normal business behaviour	Make reporting of anything that could affect security the norm. Encourage staff to report every worry, no matter how small or seemingly insignificant. This entails encouraging staff to provide the security team with information that could affect security, rather than keeping it to themselves. Initially, over-reporting will occur, but soon it will be possible to filter the noise and this will help staff get into the habit of reporting any concerns.
Make reporting easy	Ensure that reporting forms and templates do not ask for too much information upfront in case that puts people off reporting. Keep it simple and only include the minimum required information. Further investigations can uncover a more complete picture about what happened. Consider the value of a truly confidential whistleblower hotline so that people can remain anonymous.
Train people in how and why they should report	Train staff on how to report. Ideally, do this when people first start with the organisation. Also, explain why reporting is important; what it helps achieve. Reporting also needs a feedback loop so that people can understand what happened

	or what actions were taken because of their report. This acts as reinforcement for the behaviour.
Describe the reporting process on your company intranet	People need to understand what happens when they report a security incident so that they can evaluate the consequence for themselves, others and the organisation. This process should be completely transparent and outlined in simple terms on the company intranet for best effect.

HOW TO IMPROVE ORGANISATIONAL LEARNING

If you are not learning, you are going backwards. A growth and improvement mindset in organisations is critical for business, team and individual performance.

Improve organisational flexibility

Organisations need to be able to keep up with changes in security risk to ensure they can adapt quickly to changes.

Mechanism	Intervention Activities
Flexible security plan to meet changing threats	When creating a security plan, consider what is already in place before investing in additional measures. The plan should include both day-to-day arrangements and any other measures required during a heightened response period. The plan should detail protective measures to be implemented: physical, information, personnel security, security culture development, instructions on how to respond to a threat, how to respond to the discovery of a suspicious item or event, search procedures, evacuation/invacuation, business continuity plan and a communications and media strategy which includes handling enquiries from concerned family and friends (National Counter Terrorism Security Office 2014).
Identify barriers to change	Just like other risk assessments, identify what the obstacles are to achieving the security objectives in relation to change uptake or the ability to learn lessons from the past. Once identified, then strategies to minimise them can be sort. Workshops and interviews are a good way to identify barriers and come up with solutions.
If risk levels change, update policy and procedures to reflect that change.	There should be a clear line of sight from the organisation's risk assessment to its security policies and procedures. The reason for this is that staff need to understand what the basic business requirements are for security. When they do, they will be more likely to comply. Awareness programmes will be critical in this instance. This is particularly true when the security risk has increased, and therefore security needs to be tightened.

Listen to staff concerns about security

Listening is a critical leadership and management task. When we listen, we affirm that the other person and what they are saying is worthy of attention and respect. More insight into this person and the issues that affect them is gained; it also improves the quality of the relationships overall (meQuilibrium 2015). A fast way to turn people off and close down communication channels is to not listen to what they are saying.

Mechanism	Intervention Activities
Practise active listening	To actively listen to others requires the listener to do things such as: paraphrase what they have heard; repeat back to check understanding; and to ask the other person if they have understood them correctly.
Follow-up and feedback	Staff need to know who to talk to and how to report security concerns. However, security incident reporting mechanisms will not be effective if there is no feedback to the reporter about what happened as a result of their report. This is called closing the feedback loop after an incident has been reported. Staff need to feel that their report made a difference. Otherwise they won't bother to report next time.

Improve incident reporting and trend analysis

An important function of the security group is to provide management with incident reporting and trend analysis. This way increases or decreases in certain types of security incidents, and near misses can help identify emerging issues that need to be corrected.

Mechanism	Intervention Activities
Encourage the formal reporting of incidents	The reporting of incidents by staff should be encouraged. It is only through reporting and analysis thereof that the organisation can understand behavioural patterns and trends. If a reporting awareness campaign is launched, it is likely that initially the number of reports will increase. This may not mean that there are more security incidents occurring, but instead that the behaviour of reporting has increased.

How to foster continuous business improvement

Organisations who focus on continual business improvement overall are more likely to see improvements in aspects of security as a matter of course. As a minimum, organisations should encourage staff to keep up to date with security information relevant to their jobs. Seeing continuous improvement in security culture will work to prevent complacency compromising overall security objectives.

Mechanism	Intervention Activities
Analyse security events across different locations and implement mitigations across the system	Take a whole system approach to events that affect security, rather than a siloed approach. Look at events or experiences across locations and ensure they are analysed and appropriate enhancements or corrective actions implemented, not just in the one location but across the system if relevant (International Atomic Energy Agency/IAEA 2008, 14).
Conduct self-assessment and independent audits	'Conduct self-assessments and arrange for independent audits of the management systems for which they are responsible in order to identify and correct weaknesses' (IAEA 2008, 14). Self-assessments might be run by first-line staff or via second-line staff from functions such as business improvement and quality assurance. The function of self-assessments might be to identify and check control effectiveness and identify opportunities for improvement. In contrast, an audit conducted by a third party might take a deeper look into a process or policy and seek verification and evidence of compliance.
Practice drills and exercises	To improve performance in an emergency, it is important that people experience security drills and exercises first hand. An annual programme of exercises will help 'test the performance of security systems, as well as the human factor' (IAEA 2008, 14). These might be quarterly desktop or paper-based exercises with the senior management team or drills practised in a particular part of the business.
Analyse patterns and trends	Analyse patterns and trends arising from known vulnerabilities and implement action plans to mitigate poor outcomes (IAEA 2008, 14). A heat map of different types of security incidents across locations can be a good way to spot recurrent incidents in different locations.
Check compliance behaviours first hand	Observe operational performance first hand by visiting different areas of the business to confirm that expectations are being met and correct policy applied (IAEA 2008, 15). It also helps compliance behaviour if staff know that at some stage they may be checked on. This is also an effective way to observe positive security behaviours and reward staff for performing them.
Periodic reviews	'Periodically review training programmes, staff nomination and authorisation procedures, working methods, the management system, and staff access to facilities, other sensitive locations and information' (IAEA 2008, 15). This might include checking access lists for doors to sensitive areas at different locations and at different times, and user lists to databases or applications.

	Check that lists are still appropriate based on people's roles and responsibilities. It is important to verify that those who have left the organisation no longer have access and to check that those people who have moved roles still require their access levels.
Benchmark performance	'Benchmark performance to compare operations with national and international best practices' (IAEA 2008, 15). At the start of a security culture programme, it is important to establish the metrics available so that an initial benchmark for performance can be created. This is what the organisation can use to measure the programme's effectiveness. Also, it is useful to look outside the organisation to find external benchmarks. This might include looking at similar types of business to compare operations and performance. It may also include looking at international best practices coming out of industries with historically strong security cultures, such as the nuclear industry or some government organisations.
Keep up to date and use appropriate tools	As part of periodic internal reviews, it is important to maintain awareness of external security knowledge and trends. Through being aware of state-of-the-art security procedures, processes and equipment, it is possible to ensure the organisation and its staff have the appropriate tools to implement security cost effectively (IAEA 2008, 15).
Subscribe to relevant RSS feeds or social media groups	By subscribing to RSS feeds or by joining relevant groups on social media (e.g. LinkedIn groups relating to security) it is easy to keep up to date. RSS feeds summarise information from blogs, websites, news headlines, audio and video and present them to the reader in a syndicated way. This makes it easy to stay up to date on information from particular websites or many different sources.
Check websites for resources and guidance	Check relevant websites for resources and new guidance, for example: • CPNI www.cpni.gov.uk • UK National Counter Terrorism Security Office (NaCTSO) www.nactso.gov.uk • UK National Technical Authority for Information Assurance, CESG https://www.cesg.gov.uk/Pages/homepage.aspx • NZ Privacy Commissioner, Keep Safe Online https://privacy.org.nz/your-privacy/keeping-safe-online/ • NZ Department of the Prime Minister and Cabinet, Connect Smart https://www.connectsmart.govt.nz/
Attend relevant training	Encourage appropriate staff to attend relevant training courses.

Create a roadmap to close the gap between the current and desired states	Conduct an assessment or review to ascertain the current situation and the desired state. When it is clear where the gaps are, a roadmap can be created to move the organisation towards its desired state.

Mechanisms to Reward and Give Incentives for the Right Security Behaviour

Motivation, the key determinant of behaviour, is entirely dependent on the internalisation of beliefs and values. Staff performance, however, is influenced significantly by the encouragement and reinforcement received from leaders, peers and subordinates. 'Rewards and recognition, both intangible and tangible, can encourage vigilance, questioning attitudes and personal accountability' (IAEA 2008, 13–14).

HOW TO PROVIDE TANGIBLE REWARDS

'Tangible rewards are financial or non-financial rewards that can easily be assigned a financial value' (HRZone n.d.), e.g. salary, bonuses, gym memberships, discounts, flowers or other material gifts.

Give status to having a good security attitude

One way to demonstrate that an organisation promotes good security attitudes is to reward people for this as part of their formal performance management process. This status or significance can motivate employees to maintain good security behaviour as it shows the organisation thinks security is an important part of the way things are done.

Mechanism	Intervention Activities
Link performance management and promote based on having a security-conscious attitude	A useful evaluation criterion for performance management and promotion to leadership positions is whether staff display a security-conscious attitude. The way to weave this into the process is through alignment to organisational values. For example, a typical organisational value is 'professionalism'. It may be possible to link good security behaviours and having a security-conscious attitude to this or another similar value.
Communicate importance of employee's role in security	Communicate the importance of the employee's role in security. If the organisation has a reward and recognition scheme, then recognise people through this if they display good security behaviours. Public recognition is a powerful way to nurture

	desired behaviour and work satisfaction. One of the main reasons people leave organisations is because they did not feel appreciated.
Assess security performance in appraisals	Ensure that an employee's security performance is discussed at performance appraisal time. This should occur both at the end-of-year discussion as well as in quarterly catch-ups. The types of things to discuss could include their consistency in wearing their security identification pass; whether they lock their computer screen when not sitting at their computer; do they collect documents from the printer routinely after printing or leave them lying around; do they conform to the clear desk policy; and do they tidy up documents after meetings. While these behaviours relate to their own behaviour, do they also monitor and manage the security performance of others and their peers. For example, they should remind others about their obligations when they slip through correcting and coaching.
Embed security champions	When it is difficult for the security team to be everywhere and anywhere, appropriately trained and empowered security champions are a good way to provide extra capacity. The purpose of security champions is to be a local contact to provide advice in the workplace around security. They are also an excellent vehicle to provide rewards and recognition for good security behaviour. Ensure they are appropriately trained in security matters, and particular security messages and policy. Use them as a way to gauge awareness levels; provide security advice and help to staff; and encourage compliance with policy.
	The goal is to create a sense of status for the position so that people choose to be one, rather than having an extra set of duties involuntarily assigned to them.
	If you are unable to secure security champions, look at the organisation of other functions such as risk, quality or health and safety. Is it possible to leverage off these perhaps already existing positions?

Punish poor security behaviours

If there are little or no negative consequences for staff in following security policy, it will be difficult to build a strong security culture. Staff should understand that they will be reprimanded if they do not obey security rules. Action should be carried out on a consistent basis. This means that rules that apply to all staff should be enforced on all staff, including senior management.

Mechanism	Intervention Activities
Verify compliance through office and desk checks	Carry out regular office and desk checks to ensure security policy is being followed. What is done about non-compliance will depend on the organisation's appetite. If enforcement is a new concept or if a new policy is approved, it may be acceptable to just leave a note explaining the poor security behaviour and reference the rule. However, if the behaviour is unacceptable then it may be appropriate to remove the unsecured laptop, take the documents that have been left on the desk or clear out the cupboard that was left unlocked, and notify their manager. Check out what the appropriate enforcement is with senior leaders prior to conducting the office check.
Enforce disciplinary procedures and embrace opportunities to coach	Be sure to apply disciplinary procedures for security lapses consistently and visibly within a 'just culture'. That said, it is also important to consider the cause of a lapse. Is it a result of reckless behaviour, risky behaviour or resulted from human error. Reckless behaviour means that the intent was to harm, and should receive the full force of discipline. Risky behaviour does not intend to cause harm and so may require coaching initially, but repeat occurrences require discipline. Human error may require awareness and coaching or a change to the overall system to mitigate the risk further if possible. In all cases, it is a good idea to make clear the other options that were available to them and discuss how the situation can be avoided in the future. See the work of Sidney Dekker for more information on 'just culture' and balancing safety with accountability.
Pick the moment	Do not criticise, discipline or humiliate staff for security breaches in public. Ask for a word in private. Explain that you feel there is a difficulty or security issue and that a discussion would be helpful.

Use organisational reward programmes to drive performance

Use the organisation's existing reward system (e.g. salary, bonuses and benefits) to drive the desired security behaviours and outcomes.

Mechanism	Intervention Activities
Award bonuses based on good security performance	It may not be possible to have a monetary bonus purely for staff's good security behaviour. However, it may be possible to have good security performance be a factor that contributes to the staff bonus.
Give rewards for positive results of on-the-spot inspections	Make staff aware that the organisation may undertake surprise security inspections in the workplace. Give small rewards or a note of thanks for positive examples of security behaviour.

HOW TO PROVIDE INTANGIBLE REWARDS

Intangible rewards are also powerful and much cheaper motivators that are often neglected in a security context. 'Intangible rewards, such as a "thank you," "good job," or effective coaching let people know their managers care about them and value their contributions' (Sensenig 2009, 56). The other good news is that offering intangible rewards increases engagement and satisfaction, whereas withholding them has a long-term demotivation impact.

Praise staff for good security behaviour

When people feel appreciated, it can serve as a powerful motivator as they feel more connected to others and their work.

Mechanism	Intervention Activities
Customer satisfaction/ feedback surveys	Sometimes the only way to get feedback is to ask. Setting up a customer satisfaction or feedback survey is one way to receive information about performance. Be prepared for constructive criticism as well as praise.
Feedback on security performance in line management meetings	Discuss feedback on security performance in line management one-to-ones. Concentrate on both the security outcomes as well as the way people have behaved in relation to security (their qualities and attributes).
Praise each other for challenging behaviour	People are often not comfortable challenging others on their poor security behaviour or lapses. One way to make them more comfortable is to give people permission to challenge others and encourage people to thank each other after receiving feedback on their own security performance – for example, if a staff member challenges another staff member for holding the access door open for a stranger without a security pass. Encourage the employee who was in the wrong to thank the other staff member for challenging them.
How to give praise and appreciation	There is a method for giving sincere praise and appreciation designed by Kevin Sensenig of Dale Carnegie & Associates that brings out the best in people. This method is described below:
	Step 1: Tell them what you appreciate about them. Say, for example: 'John, what I really appreciate about you is that you're a very good at ensuring the information you have with you when travelling is protected.' Step 2: Give evidence. Say, for example: 'The reason I say that is because I have seen you upload the information to an encrypted memory stick so that if you lose it, it cannot be compromised. This tells me that you're engaged in security and take the necessary steps to protect this organisation from privacy breaches.'

	Step 3: Ask an open-ended question. 'The natural response to step 2 would be for an employee to return the favo[u]r by saying something nice about the manager who is paying the compliment. However, that is not the desired outcome in this format. The idea is to let the employee absorb the appreciation being given. So the next step is to ask an open-ended question. For example, "How did you develop such good [security] skills?" Let the individual talk about experiences and jobs that have helped him develop his professional character. This keeps the focus of the appreciation on the person.' (Sensenig 2009, 57)

Recognise staff for good security behaviour

The line managers and the organisation should regularly and publicly recognise individuals and teams who do a good job in security.

Mechanism	Intervention Activities
Regularly recognise good approaches to security	Display the good security performance of employees on the notice board. Recognise people for their behaviour in team meetings. Include employees' names in the organisation's newsletter. Announce the 'security employee of the month' or 'security employee of the year'.

Provide performance feedback

The role of performance feedback on the job is vital. Without feedback, people do not understand what to do, how they are doing it, why they are doing it or that they can do it. Timely feedback can be a powerful motivator, helps people understand the impact of their behaviour, and gives them a chance to improve.

Mechanism	Intervention Activities
Give regular feedback	Give regular feedback on the security aspects of their work. This can be done informally through on-the-job coaching or formally via regular catch-ups as part of performance management. While negative feedback has a place, also ensure that positive feedback is given about what they have done well.

Provide development of security knowledge and skills

Staff personal development should explicitly include developing security knowledge, awareness and skills. This then shows that the organisation gives performance development in this area serious and due attention.

Mechanism	Intervention Activities
Add security awareness to performance appraisals	At the time of the appraisal, check that staff have undergone awareness training or refreshers where appropriate.
Support staff development in security	Ensure there is support for staff development in relation to security knowledge, awareness and skills. For example, support staff in attending internal and external security training, conferences, lunchtime seminars and networking groups and other related initiatives.
Help managers develop their teams' security awareness	Help managers and their employees develop their security culture and awareness. Perhaps it is possible to give briefings to their team on security or develop eLearning packages for the organisation. Think about what quick reference material staff may find helpful, e.g. pamphlets on how to correctly classify information or how to handle information when mobile. Ask staff what information would be handy to have at their fingertips to help them conform to security policy.
Track and record security awareness training	Ensure that any security awareness training that staff have undergone is monitored and recorded.
Give staff the security training they need to do their jobs	For example, train HR recruitment staff in personnel security matters such as security vetting and dealing with behaviours of concern in the workplace. Send a communications and marketing staff member on a security basics course so that they can better meet the security communications design needs through better understanding of the security function. Ensure IT security employees are current on the emerging cyber security threats from a technical and business perspective.

HOW TO EMPOWER EMPLOYEES IN RELATION TO SECURITY

People like to have their ideas heard. Empowering people by giving them decision-making authority, making them feel like their ideas are welcomed, and providing autonomy is a good way to motivate staff in relation to security.

Provide management support

Management should demonstrate that they will back staff up if they stop a job for security reasons.

Mechanism	Intervention Activities
Give staff tools to make difficult decisions	Richard Branson and others have suggested some tips for making difficult decisions (Feloni 2014). Simple models such as these may help staff make and feel confident about difficult security decisions. 1. Don't act on an emotional response – take the time to settle down and find data before letting your feelings control you. 2. Find as many downsides to a problem as possible – consider everything that could go wrong before moving forward. 3. Look at the big picture – look at how the decision will affect other projects in the short and long term. 4. Protect the downside – limit losses before moving forward.
Publically acknowledge those who make difficult security decisions	Publically acknowledge staff who have had to make difficult security decisions in meetings or via email.

Delegate security responsibility

Delegating is a valuable management tool that can be used to motivate employees by providing them with a feeling of ownership and responsibility. It also helps employees develop for the benefit of the organisation.

Mechanism	Intervention Activities
Provide delegation training	Delegation is effective if done well, but can also be detrimental if done poorly, causing reduced quality, reduced productivity and frustration. Therefore, it is beneficial to provide delegation training for managers in relation to security to ensure the right tasks are delegated to the right person, with the right direction.
Successful delegation guidelines	To delegate for best effect, there are a few simple things that should be considered.

1. Ensure the task is appropriate to be delegated. For example, your core functions or responsibilities should not be delegated otherwise your value will be diminished.

2. Ensure the person you are delegating to is either capable of completing the task or is provided with the right level of coaching and support.

3. Be transparent about why the task is being delegated and communicate this to the person you are delegating to, but also to others who need to know.

4. Be explicit in defining the outcome to be achieved – what does 'good' look like when this task is completed?

5. Define when the task needs to be completed by and what priority it has as opposed to their other work.

6. Check in on them and give them opportunities to ask further questions.

7. Provide feedback on how well the task is being performed as required.

Give staff formal responsibilities for security

It is important that staff realise they all have a role to play in maintaining security. While the security team should have oversight for security, they are not accountable for security. Implementation and accountability resides with staff who are the first line of defence.

Mechanism	Intervention Activities
Job description responsibilities	Include security responsibilities in job descriptions. An example could be 'ensure staff understand, respect and remain vigilant in following organisational policies and procedures' (Root n.d). Managers should make certain employees understand what this responsibility looks like in the workplace and what behaviours are expected to satisfy this responsibility.

| Clarify security responsibilities | Clarify security responsibilities through discussions between manager and employee to check they understand their responsibilities. |

Organisational Systems as Mechanisms to Shape Security Culture

Staff performance is influenced by the quality of organisational systems and the provision of expectations, requirements and standards for work, training, documented procedures, information systems and so on. Therefore, a well-developed management system is an essential feature of effective security. Organisational systems must be put in place so that expectations are defined; to implement and define processes; to measure progress and assess compliance; to improve performance on the basis of experience, and to manage change.

HOW TO PUT IN PLACE THE 'RIGHT' POLICIES, PROCEDURES AND PROCESSES

Policies, procedures and processes help employees understand the rules and behaviour expected of them in the workplace. It should be easy for staff to work out what the 'right' behaviour is.

Clear expectations about how to handle a security incident

If a security incident occurs, there will be certain things an organisation may want staff to do, in a particular order. Therefore, it is important that staff know what to do if an incident occurs.

Mechanism	Intervention Activities
Include the handling of security breaches in induction and training	Many businesses conduct mandatory induction training for all new employees. Security induction is vital because the vigilance of *all* staff (from cleaning and maintenance to contract staff) is

	essential to the security of the business. Ensure that information about what is expected of individuals is included in inductions and training – e.g. wearing security passes and challenging those without passes; not sharing passwords or security access; managing sensitive information; reporting suspicious behaviour and security issues. Direct staff to where they can find out more about security policies and procedures. All employees' personal records should be endorsed as evidence that they have received this training.
Utilise lists	Have lists available for staff to follow for security incidents so that it is clear what needs to be done and it is easy to do it. Print lists onto wallet-sized cards so that they can be kept on them at all times.

Fit for purpose policy and procedures

Policies and procedures should be kept up to date and reviewed annually to ensure they are fit for purpose. If policies are not fit for purpose, then there is a risk that they will be ignored completely.

Mechanism	Intervention Activities
Have a visible policy document	Ensure that a security policy is established for the organisation and posted in facilities and offices, and that it is familiar to staff. The policy document needs to state the organisation's commitment to security. It should establish the highest expectations for decision-making and conduct, and should be supported by an atmosphere of professionalism in the security field. '[T]here is a particular need to ensure that [employees] understand that adherence to the policy is expected of all [staff]. These expectations include protecting information, being aware of potential security concerns and threats, and being vigilant in reporting security incidents. These general expectations can be established through a documented code of conduct' (IAEA 2008, 22).

Have a code of conduct	Ensure a staff code of conduct exists which covers the need for security, and make sure employees 'are familiar with the code of conduct through ongoing training and awareness' (IAEA 2008, 23). For example: • Is it acceptable to leave staff laptops unsecured? • Is it acceptable to leave visitors unsupervised? • Is it acceptable to leave printouts on the printer overnight? • Is there any particular level of information that needs to be encrypted rather than unencrypted in transit?
Make policies simple and easy to adopt	Make it easier for security procedures to be adopted by creating clear policies. Ensure procedures inform staff about exactly what they can and can't do in relation to security.
Use staff discussions to identify barriers to following procedures	Use staff discussions to identify the top three security procedures that get in the way of people doing their job. Share these amongst the group and get them into solution mode so that they brainstorm together a way forward.
Identify which procedures are easy to implement and why	Staff may be more likely to follow some security procedures over others. Find out why some procedures are easy to comply with, and use that information in the creation of new procedures or in improvement of existing difficult ones.

Consistency of application of security practices

To enable uniformity in the application of security practices, there should be clarity about exactly what is expected and this should be role modelled and enforced.

Mechanism	Intervention Activities
Lead from the front	Ensure senior leaders lead from the front. Senior managers should model the way for staff so that they understand good security practices, such as locking laptops and papers away at the end of the day, security pass wearing and using encrypted memory sticks. Senior leaders should also challenge people who are not following policy to show that it is important. The phrase 'what you permit, you promote' applies here.
Hold a security amnesty	Security amnesties are a good way to promote a policy and make it alright for staff to return equipment they don't need (or has been left behind by staff who have left the company) or to own up to security inconsistencies without fear of being punished. Examples of security amnesties are:

	• to declare system or database access you should not have;
	• for USB sticks that are no longer needed or that are unencrypted;
	• for unowned laptops that are taking up space in cupboards;
	• for access cards that are no longer needed.

HOW TO ENSURE THE SECURITY COMPETENCE OF STAFF

Staff need to feel that they are competent to undertake their security responsibilities.

Include security as part of staff performance appraisals

When security issues are part of an individual's appraisal, it is possible to identify and address any training needs.

Mechanism	Intervention Activities
Security as part of performance appraisal	Have staff security performance as a mandatory element of performance appraisals. If it is not possible to give security its own section on the appraisal, link it to a discussion about the organisational values and employee behaviour.
Provide scripts to managers for appraisals	Provide managers with scripted questions or sentences that will enable them to bring up security issues during appraisals.

Assess the performance of the security programme, including awareness

Ensure objective measures or KPIs are in place to measure security programme performance.

Mechanism	Intervention Activities
Create a security quiz or survey	A security quiz or survey is a good way to understand security awareness levels.
Use security metrics	The security department, like any other organisational group, should be held accountable for its performance. To manage a security programme correctly, its performance must be measured using metrics. See Chapter 7 for more on choosing appropriate security metrics.

| Create a Security Balanced Scorecard or dashboard to present performance | Show the security department's performance in a useful and businesslike way using a Security Balanced Scorecard or security dashboard (see Chapter 7). |

Include security in induction packages

It is important that security issues are included in inductions and have enough time allocated to them. Inductions set the scene about what is expected in the workplace and are an ideal time to influence the behaviour of staff.

Mechanism	Intervention Activities
Work with HR	Work with HR to establish what they consider the optimum amount of content during induction that should be spent on security issues.
Provide engaging security induction materials	Employees are often overloaded with new information during inductions, so ensure that security awareness materials are simple and as engaging as possible.
Use short videos to convey key messages	Consider including a short video about security issues in the induction. There are professional security awareness videos that are available online that could be incorporated into security training like the ones that CPNI publishes on YouTube at https://www.youtube.com/user/UKCPNI. These also cover a range of topics such as keeping safe online, personnel security and general security awareness.

ORGANISATIONAL GOVERNANCE AND BUSINESS STRATEGY

Over time it is natural that governance requirements and business strategies will change as the organisation grows, changes and matures. This section is about how an organisation manages those changes as they relate to security.

Project management and planning

All work must be suitably planned to ensure that security is not compromised and implementation is going smoothly.

Mechanism	Intervention Activities
Ensure implementers have project management and change management skills	Project and change management skills should not be overlooked in security changes. Proper planning, scheduling and communication to stakeholders are vital to ensure effective change.

Learn lessons from previous security changes	If formal 'lessons learnt' documentation does not exist, then ask about previous implementations of security measures. Find out what worked well and what didn't and why. Review the information with a view to improving implementation in the future.
Incorporate security issues into long-term business planning	Security issues should be incorporated into long-term business planning so that the organisation is not playing catch-up if the need to change security procedures arises suddenly. It also pays to have a contingency fund in place in case there are any unforeseen eventualities.
Approval for deviations	Staff should 'follow the established plans or seek proper approval to deviate from planned duties and activities' (IAEA 2008, 25).
Detailed planning	'Work [should be] planned in sufficient detail to allow staff to work effectively and efficiently (e.g. resources are matched to demands, spare parts and tools are available when needed)' (IAEA 2008, 25).
Interfaces between workgroups	'The interfaces [and interdependencies] between workgroups [should be] considered and addressed during planning' (IAEA 2008, 25).
Security risk management planning	Does the risk management plan include acts of terrorism in addition to normal risk management for flood, fire and low-level crime? For example, does it include a bomb call plan; a systematic search programme for suspect items; a routine bomb evacuation plan? The best way to manage protective security hazards and risks to the business is first to understand and identify the threats and vulnerabilities. Then identify any improvements needed and the security and contingency plans to be developed. For some businesses, simple good practice coupled with a good security culture (staff vigilance) and well-exercised contingency arrangements may be all that is needed (National Counter Terrorism Security Office 2014).
Contingency planning	Contingency plans to address foreseeable events should be established and regularly tested (IAEA 2008). Making this part of the way the business is run, rather than having to firefight any emergency, helps prepare the organisation to offer business as usual in the quickest time possible.

How to ensure people know who to tell about security issues

Staff need to know who to ask and inform about security issues so that they can be tackled appropriately.

Mechanism	Intervention Activities
Communicate the security contact(s) to staff	Put signs up in and around the office (e.g. in the kitchen, by the printer, in the corridors) with the names of the security team and their contact details. Ensure these details are easy to find on your company intranet and communicate them regularly at meetings where appropriate.
Promote security contacts alongside other similar contacts	Consider promoting the names of those to approach about security issues alongside those responsible for other issues such as risk management, quality and H&S.
Find ways to make remembering the security contacts memorable	Find ways to make remembering the security contacts memorable. For example, turn remembering the contacts into a competition with a prize; embed the names into a crossword puzzle; or have them as a question on a security quiz night.

Workforce planning (WFP)

It is necessary to have sufficient people resources to ensure that security is sustained satisfactorily.

Mechanism	Intervention Activities
Embed security roles in the organisation	If it is not possible to increase headcount in the security team itself, consider giving staff around the business a specific security role to play in addition to their regular role. You might call these people security representatives, security champions or security coordinators. Their function, once trained, is to assist with security initiatives and help and guide staff on their security issues.
Identify WFP shortfalls	Identify what the security people resource issues are and plan to have them rectified in the next year's budgeting so that headcount meets requirements.

Ensure change management is carried out properly

'Change is, at its core, a people process.' Many change efforts fail as 'they do not capture the hearts and minds of the people who need to operate differently to deliver the change' (Harshak et al. 2010, 5). As the requirements for the organisation change, it is important that staff are informed about any changes promptly. If they do not find out in time and it affects their ability to do their role, negative feedback will ensue.

Mechanism	Intervention Activities
Change management processes	Put processes in place to deal with changes that could affect security (IAEA 2008). Ensure that security is considered as a matter of course as part of a project risk register or risk assessment process.
Coordinated change management	Changes in areas such as operations, security and safety should be coordinated with all potentially affected stakeholders (IAEA 2008). This requires identifying who the internal and external stakeholders are and communicating the change to them from the scoping phase all the way through to implementation. It is also important to be aware of other changes happening within the business so that the amount of change affecting these areas is considered. If too much change is occurring at once then operations, security or safety is likely to be compromised. Large amounts of change may require proper scheduling so that only one or two changes occur each week for example.
Risk assess changes	Assessments should be made to ensure that changes have achieved the desired outcomes and have not affected security procedures (IAEA 2008). Is a security risk case required? This is a documented review of the proposed change to see if risk levels have changed or other risks created. A risk assessment might be necessary when: • a control measure no longer minimises the risk so far as is reasonably practicable; • a new security risk is identified; • consultation with members of the workforce indicates that a review is necessary; • a trained security representative or champion requests a review (where they reasonably believe that any of the above mentioned circumstances may affect the security of the organisation's assets – people, information or physical – and the organisation has not conducted a review in response).
Have a regular security communication update process	What is the best way for your organisation to share important security messages? Consider using one or all of these possible communication mechanisms: all-staff emails; notices on the company intranet; posters; text messages; quarterly videos of the CEO or an executive security sponsor.

Prioritise the sharing of critical security updates	If there are too many security communications, then the critical ones will be lost in the crowd. Consider what criteria your organisation should use to prioritise key security messages, e.g. the level of impact on services, customers, reputation or legal and regulatory factors.
Understand and spell out the impact of change on people	Know the positives for individuals (what's in it for me?) as well as the negatives (what's against my interests?). This can help build the case for change and help employees understand what the change means for them: • Why are we changing? • What is changing; what is staying the same? • What are the benefits? This also provides the basis for communicating with staff about the change (Harshak et al. 2010).

Mechanisms to Manage Business and Organisational Pressures

'Employers have responsibilities [for] both statutory and common law for the health, safety and welfare of their employees' (Bagshaw n.d.). This section deals with how to enhance the capacity of staff to manage pressure more positively, and to build their resilience to stress and fatigue. It also discusses the business pressures in organisations that can either hinder or enhance security-conscious behaviour.

LOOK AFTER EMPLOYEE WELFARE

When an organisation shows concern for the personal welfare of its staff (e.g. working conditions, safety, sick leave), they have a more positive view of the organisation and are then more likely to attend to security alongside other organisational aims.

Mechanism	Intervention Activities
Demonstrate concern for staff personal welfare by	• Ensure staff have the right equipment/clothing (PPE) and training needed to do the work and that it is maintained sufficiently. • Make certain that staff have a safe working environment or that appropriate mitigation is put in place. • Encourage staff to take sick leave if they are unwell and to use their annual leave during the year it accrues.

	• Put in place a wellbeing programme to help staff be more healthy and productive at work. • Ensure the environment is conducive to high standards of work or security performance (e.g. housekeeping, timely provision of tools/equipment). • Consult staff about the ergonomics and effectiveness of their work environment. • Ensure that the text of guides and procedures is user-friendly and understandable to staff. • Encourage senior managers to visit staff regularly, especially during periods of reduced activity such as back shifts, late shifts and weekends.

Consider work–life balance

Staff's levels of work–life balance are important in any context, but also in the security context. An imbalance, weighted more heavily to work rather than life, can act to disengage people and feelings of resentment can follow. This could cause them to cut corners to get a job completed or on purpose due to more risk-taking behaviour.

Mechanism	Intervention Activities
Ensure managers have regular catch-ups	Managers should have regular catch-up sessions with their subordinates about how they are doing and feeling about work. These sorts of personal interactions create trust far quicker than by phone, email, or messages via the intranet.
Adopt a coaching role	Have managers employ a coaching position with their subordinates to help identify ways in which they can continue to ensure that security does not interfere with their personal lives. For example: Help employees identify their unique strengths and weaknesses and link them to personal and career aspirations. Encourage employees to establish a long-term plan for achieving them. (Goleman 2000, 87)

How to ensure fatigue does not hinder security practices

A tired employee may disregard security practices, and so it is important to consider how this can be mitigated.

Mechanism	Intervention Activities
Promote importance of rest and encourage staff to take breaks	Promote the importance of taking opportunities to rest and take breaks. Resting and having fun is a basic human need. It is now recognised that working long and hard at something you do not enjoy is a recipe for burnout. Suggest that employees put some enjoyment back into their day and tell them not to feel guilty about taking a 'fun' break. Is there a way to make the current situation more bearable or fun, to help staff freshen up and, therefore, increase their ability to maintain security?
Peer and line manager supervision	People will often push through their fatigue barriers out of a sense of duty or pure determination. It is, therefore, important that both peers and line managers provide some level of supervision to ensure people are managing their energy levels appropriately.

How to ensure stress does not hinder security practices

Not unlike when there is an imbalance between work and life, the amount of pressure or stress people experience can cause staff to become disengaged and, therefore, less motivated to comply with security policy.

Mechanism	Intervention Activities
Avoid complicated procedures	Avoid complicated procedures that might frustrate employees and make their job harder than it needs to be. Clear and concise procedures outlining what needs to be done will help ensure they are followed.
Train managers in health and wellbeing	Train managers in health and wellbeing so that they have an awareness of the indicators and signs of stress, pressure and depression. Armed with this knowledge they may be more likely to pick up on stress in the workplace and be able to help employees find the support they need before the situation becomes more difficult.

| Regular catch-ups with staff about work and wellbeing | Ensure managers have regular catch-ups with their staff to find out how they are coping with matters such as workload, work prioritisation, inter-office dynamics and general wellbeing. Areas to check include:

• Health and fitness – stress brings physical strain, but we can cope better if we have good health and fitness levels.

• Social support – this includes all the groups we belong to (family, friends and colleagues); they are an invaluable source of companionship, moral and practical support and suggestions.

• Skills and experience – our experience of past changes may help us deal with current changes; we can use skills like time-management to make our situation easier.

• Property and finance – a more difficult area for a manager to check, but not having these resources, is an area of stress. Having them can help ease our situation, perhaps by paying people to help, or taking a holiday. |

Show concern for health and wellbeing

Organisations should have a sensible approach to employee health and wellbeing. Healthy employees cost less than unhealthy ones, and employees are more likely stay with the company due to the wellness programme (Berry et al. 2010).

Mechanism	Intervention Activities
Show concern for health and wellbeing	One way to show concern for people's health and wellbeing is to start one-to-one meetings with questions about how the employee is and how their family are. These are usually good openers into how things are going at home or how much energy people feel they have. They also have the advantage of softening up a conversation and are a good way to check in with people.
Encourage employees to take breaks	Watch out for employees who rarely take breaks from their work. While their intentions may be good, their concentration and quality of work is certain to drop, and they are also not doing their wellbeing any good. There is a lot of good research out there now about the negative side effects of sitting down for extended periods of time. In fact, some indications are that it is as bad for your health as smoking. One large research study 'found that compared with those who sat the least, people who sat the longest had a:

	• 112% increase in risk of diabetes
	• 147% increase in cardiovascular events
	• 90% increase in death caused by cardiovascular events
	• 49% increase in death from any cause' (NHS 2014).
Promote regular exercise	A good way to promote exercise in the workplace is to set up walking meetings – a particular time slot during the day where the meeting is held while on a walk around a few blocks. This encourages a more informal tone to the meeting and often increased dialogue. It also provides an excellent way to exercise and clear the mind before heading back to the office.
	Another way to encourage exercise in the workplace is to allow people to finish work 30 or 45 minutes early, granted that they are going off to do some exercise there and then.
Use 'caring' to your advantage	The presence of individuals affects our thinking and decision-making more than we realise, or perhaps, wish to admit. In a study by Paul Slovic into charitable giving, he ran two parallel approaches in requesting donations on behalf of Save the Children. One approach gave statistics on the millions of starving children while the other was simply accompanied by a photo of a single starving child. The approach with the individual child received 50% more in donations (Williams 2012).
	Take opportunities to personalise your security risks where possible. Are there examples of a particular risk affecting someone personally? For example, if a new privacy policy is brought in, can you draw attention to anyone whose identity was stolen or personal information misused? This may help influence staff behaviour and compliance with that policy.

UNDERSTAND THE POWER OF PEER PRESSURE

Peer pressure refers to the desire we experience to conform. It is a significant motivator of behaviour and it affects you more than you think. This is particularly true when you are in an in-group, such as you are when you join an organisation.

Expecting colleagues to behave in the right way

At work, like in other situations, we are expected to behave in certain ways. In a security context, particularly in an organisation with a strong security culture, we might expect our peers to follow security policy and procedures. If they don't, then we might lean on them a bit, and apply peer pressure, to bring them back into line. But even in organisations with weak security culture, peer pressure can be used to manage the behaviour of others and motivate them to follow the correct procedures.

Mechanism	Intervention Activities
Employ a buddy system	Buddy systems are a useful vehicle to ensure that people are following policies correctly, particularly for new employees.
Allocate security responsibilities to the team to check each other	Individuals are much more likely to take responsibility if they are designated a role; they are more comfortable if they have been told to do something. For example, get staff to check their team members' desks if they are the last to leave to ensure that laptops are locked away and confidential papers are not left out insecurely.
Promote a good security environment vision and get the team to sign up to it	Teams can create for themselves a vision of how they wish to behave in relation to security and what type of positive security environment they want to work in. Get buy-in to the vision and this will increase trust amongst colleagues that they will adhere to security procedures.
Develop a challenge culture	The best way to develop a challenge culture is to give staff standard phrases that open up a conversation about the security issue they have seen. For example, if someone is found walking around without a security pass or escort ask them 'You look lost, can I help you?' If someone has left documents in a meeting room, then say 'I noticed you left these behind. I picked them up so that they don't get into the wrong hands.' If someone has left their computer screen unlocked while away from their desk, leave them a note telling them you noticed their screen was unlocked while they were away so you locked it for them. This is even more powerful when challenging is role modelled by senior management.
Peer reinforcement	Encourage peers to reinforce behaviour that enhances security.
Personal responsibility to resolve issues	Encourage staff to take personal responsibility for resolving security issues. Encourage a solution focus, rather than problem focus to issues.

Foster a positive attitude to security rules

Staff should perceive security as an essential part of their work. The best way to promote this is to generate a positive attitude to security. Just like feelings of negative downward spirals, it is possible to generate positive upward spirals. The benefit of positive attitudes and upward spirals in matters like security are that people can see and think of more possibilities and options to solve whatever problem they face. They are also more likely to take action, develop long-term plans and goals and show increased resilience.

Mechanism	Intervention Activities
Explain the benefits of security to staff	Help staff to see the positive benefits of security measures by messaging these in regular communications. For example, it may be frustrating that a particular IT application is down for an hour, but the benefit is that the necessary security patches will mean it is more reliable in the future.
Provide alternative ways forward; don't just say no	The security team are often tasked with restricting people from doing things they want to do. Instead of saying no, provide them with different options and explain the benefits or costs to themselves and the organisation, of each. The goal is to have them going away understanding the need for and remaining positive to security.

Do not share security access

Not sharing security passes or computer logins and passwords are key elements of maintaining effective security. The danger in sharing access is that those unique passes and logins act as a sort of signature. If more than one person uses the same details, it is difficult to verify who has done what. It also puts the facility or system at risk of those details being shared more widely with people who are not authorised by the organisation. There can be an element of social pressure to either share passwords in organisations with weak security culture or pressure not to share passwords in organisations with strong security cultures. The aim is to have social pressure tipping towards the not sharing direction.

Mechanism	Intervention Activities
Explain the implications of sharing access	To get staff to buy into not sharing access, there is a need to explain the implications of doing so to them.
Give staff the security access they need	Give staff the security access they need to do their job. No more, no less. For example, visitors should be escorted and should wear clearly marked temporary passes; contract and agency staff should be provided with photo passes once their identity is established as genuine. Insist that the pass be worn at all times. Anyone not displaying a security pass should be challenged or reported immediately to security or management.

Encourage staff to contact the security group before sharing access	Encourage staff to contact the security group if they think they may have to share access. The security group may be able to offer another solution, even if temporary until the situation is resolved.

Foster the right cultural norms

Embedding the right cultural norms in the organisation will make the difference as to whether employees who delay a job for the sake of security are seen as difficult or they are perceived as professional. If people are viewed as difficult, this will not encourage people to make the right decisions in terms of security and the delivery of their work.

Mechanism	Intervention Activities
Appreciate and recognise	Anyone who raises a security concern should be provided with appreciation. There may also be an opportunity to recognise publically their professional and prosocial behaviour.
Make the right decisions regarding security	Employees need to feel they will be supported if they raise security concerns, no matter if it may mean an impact on time, scope or cost.
Pygmalion effect	Our expectations of others shape our behaviour towards them, which in turn affects how they behave towards us. If you treat staff and their behaviour as you believe they should act and behave, rather than how they do now, they will come closer to the ideal and the behaviour you want (Williams 2012).

UTILISE THE RULE OF RECIPROCITY TO INFLUENCE SECURITY BEHAVIOURS

The rule of reciprocity is a type of social norm which can have a powerful influence on our behaviour. Have you ever felt obliged to do something for someone because they have first done something for you? This is a fundamental human need to return positive actions with positive actions. We feel obligated to return favours to others who have done favours for us. David Strohmetz conducted one of many studies on this phenomenon of tipping, and the age-old tradition of offering a sweet with the bill. Compared to offering no sweets, one sweet resulted in a 3% increase in average tips; two sweets showed a 14% increase. The best result came via a slight twist on the technique. Offering a single sweet at first but then adding a 'bonus' sweet as if it were a last-minute favour, scored a 23% increase in tips (Strohmetz 2002). This principle could also be used to encourage the right security behaviours in staff.

Mechanism	Intervention Activities
The 'that's not all' technique	This method is commonly used in sales pitches: a salesperson tells the audience the price of an item and then throws something else in for free. It appears as if they are doing you a favour or conceding something by offering an additional item that was not requested (Cherry n.d. [a]). Try using the technique in these situations: • Persuade a manager to send his staff on security training courses by offering to do a security risk assessment of their area for free. • Ask to brief the team at the next meeting on a certain security subject, e.g. on the refreshed security policy, and offer to bring cakes for them to enjoy while they listen.
Offer something for free in return for listening to your security message	When someone gives you something, we often feel a need to return the favour and give them something too. The next time you are trying to convey a certain security message and need to persuade someone to listen, offer the person or group something for free – perhaps some security awareness merchandise (e.g. pens, mousepads, calendars and so on). This may create a feeling of obligation for the receiver that may help the security cause (Cherry n.d.[b]).
The door-in-the-face strategy	Think about a time when someone made a large request of you. It was probably easy in that instance to say no (or to 'slam the door in their face'). However, if they then make a much smaller request, human psychology suggests that we are more likely to say yes (Cherry n.d.[b]). Try using this strategy in these scenarios: • First ask if all of the group can be sent on security training (e.g. awareness, information security practices, personal data handling, identity vetting). If the manager says no to all their staff going on training, ask if a smaller number can attend. • When trying to push through a change, e.g. the acceptance of a protective marking scheme, ask that all the organisation's documents are protectively marked with labels. If the senior team turn down that proposal, propose marking only confidential or sensitive documents.

The paying it forward strategy	Paying it forward is a more positive, less scheming, way to use the rule of reciprocity. It means exactly what it sounds like, you be the first to offer something, make a compromise or do something kind for someone else (Cherry n.d.[b]).
	This concerns prosocial behaviours you might use to inspire reciprocal acts of kindness, discretionary effort and positive security behaviours. For example:
	• locking away a colleague's laptop if they have forgotten to do so;
	• clearing sensitive documents off someone's desk so they avoid being reprimanded during an office inspection from the security group;
	• offering to help a colleague who is struggling with something;
	• If you notice someone with login's and passwords written on scraps of paper and in notebooks, introduce them to an online password manager – a secure vault for storing and managing shared sensitive information such as passwords, documents and digital identities (help set it up for added kudos).
Resisting reciprocity	Understanding how the rule of reciprocity works means that you can know recognise when it may be being used on you. If you find yourself in this predicament, it is possible to resist this psychological principal by doing the following (Cherry n.d[b]):
	• Don't give a response straight away. It can beneficial to give a holding statement such as 'I'll get back to you on that' or 'I need to think about it some more' as the desire to reciprocate is strongest at first and then reduces over time.
	• Consider the value of the initial gift as opposed to the request being made. Are they of equal value? Often the gift is of much smaller value compared to the request.

HOW TO AVOID CONFLICTING GOALS

Conflicting goals between maintaining security and getting work done should be prevented where possible. People may have good intentions of following security policy; however, when they come under pressure from things like workload issues, they may choose not to comply with security if they see it as conflicting with their ability to get things done in time.

How to reduce complacency and apathy

Complacency or apathy should not hinder the maintenance of security. The importance of following security at all times should be highlighted.

Mechanism	Intervention Activities
Train staff on how to avoid work goal conflicts	When rolling out a new security procedure or a revised policy, this can be a good time to ensure that staff are trained appropriately and understand what they need to do to maintain security even when work goals conflict.
Emphasise importance of security for the business	Never miss an opportunity to emphasise the importance of security to the organisation. Good times for it to be mentioned might be at the start of all staff meetings, in team or line manager meetings, or as a message on the company intranet.
Use checklists	The reason airline pilots use checklists is to avoid complacency. Checklists are a good way to ensure that all necessary steps are carried out. They break a task down into more memorable chunks that are readily remembered. The types of checklist that can be used in a security content are: • Lists of things a staff member should do before they leave work to go home. For example, 1) ensure desk is clear; 2) ensure pedestal is locked; 3) check printer is clear and turned off; 4) check that team members have done so as well. • Lists of things to do before leaving a meeting room. For example, 1) rub off any information written on the whiteboard; 2) clear desk of papers that have been left behind (or remind others not to leave them behind); 3) log out of any computers used. • Lists of things to do before locking up the office. For example, 1) check staff have cleared their desk, locked their computers and locked information away; 2) check printer is clear and put any printed papers in the bins for secure disposal; 3) check windows are closed and locked; 4) turn all lights off; and 5) lock the door and set the alarm.

Look out for repeated security breaches	If the same types of breach are occurring more than once, it may be an opportunity to review the design of the policy, the procedure or system. There may be another way it can be designed which might stop the breaches occurring altogether. We can also leverage near misses as much as possible. They should be framed as a 'close call' rather than a false alarm. Seize upon the emotion and dissonance after an event. Draw attention to recent and nearby events also.
Security awareness videos	As part of an awareness campaign, use short videos that focus on complacency, to illustrate to staff the dangers of not following procedures. Check out CPNI UK's channel on YouTube for free security awareness videos (https://www.youtube.com/user/UKCPNI).
Tell a story	Using an engaging story to explain high levels of risk is a good way to help employees remember why they need to follow procedures. The story of Rick Rescorla, Security Director of Morgan Stanley in the World Trade Center, is a powerful example of the importance of emergency drill rehearsal. Rescorla successful evacuated most of his firm's 2,687 employees in the September 11, 2011 attacks, but then lost his own life. This is a story that is worth looking up on the internet.
Use visible endorsements of preparation from leadership	Senior management should show their support for preventative security measures and the preparation that has gone into what to do in the event of a breach.
Target the 'most likely' and 'most dangerous' risks	It is important to pitch the most believable and viable threats. Therefore, target the 'most likely' and 'most critical' security issues and risks to avoid being viewed as 'crying wolf'. Plan effectively for a variety of reasonable scenarios.
Tailor the message to the audience	Always consider the 'persona' of the audience in security risk communications. Personas are the archetypal users of a service or product that represents the needs of larger user groups in terms of goals and personal characteristics. Although personas are fictitious, they are based on knowledge of real users. User research is conducted before personas are written to ensure they represent the end users rather than the opinion of the writer. Typical personas might include 'Business Risk Owner', 'Operations Manager' or 'IT Manager', and security incidents will mean different things to each of them. For example: If considering what systems being compromised means to them: 1. IT Manager – cyber incident 2. Operational Manager – systems and procedures interrupted 3. Business Risk Owner – reputational damage (loss of market confidence).

	If considering what an electronic theft means to them: 1. IT Manager – systems breached 2. Operations Manager – unprotected systems, customer information stolen 3. Business Risk Owner – reputational damage (loss of customer confidence) If considering what online services overloaded means to them: 1. IT Manager – Distributed Denial of Service (DDOS) 2. Operational Manager – customers cannot place orders (e-commerce impact) 3. Business Risk Owner – financial damage (loss of sales) Personas identify user motivations, expectations and goals responsible for driving behaviour. Knowing these means that language and approach can be tailored to best influence behaviour (Petersen 2012).

Do not let pressure of time or delivery hinder security

In a weak security culture, when people are under pressure to deliver or have deadlines to meet they may look to cut corners or take shortcuts, particularly if they think no one is looking. This is detrimental to security and it should be regularly communicated that this is unacceptable. However, if staff do find themselves in this position, then they should speak to the security department to understand what options are available to them.

Mechanism	Intervention Activities
Include security in scoping phase	Ensure security is considered in the scoping of any work or project so that security aspects can be factored into the timeline.
Appreciate and recognise	Appreciate and recognise those who follow security procedures even when deadlines are pressing.
Communicate the message to staff	As part of the security awareness programme, the importance of following security rules even when under work pressures might be a good key message to focus on. Consider a month-long campaign on this topic.
Staff to share ideas for improvement/build an ethic of contribution	Provide open communication channels for employees to share ideas about how best to ensure security practices are followed no matter the time pressure. Encourage staff to look beyond their specific roles and advance the common purpose. The ethic of contribution means going beyond one's formal responsibilities to solve broader problems, not just applying greater effort (Williams 2012).

PAUSE for thought	Even the most difficult conflicts between time pressure and security maintenance can be worked out, but the key is to 'PAUSE':
	Pause before launching into a tirade and disciplining staff.
	Attend to conflicts early.
	Understand each other's world.
	Seek win-win solutions.
	Emphasise future opportunities, such as coming to the security team first to discuss conflicts and time pressures.
Security representative on project working groups	Having a security representative involved in project working groups is a good way to ensure security is given due consideration. This person would help to ensure that the security aspects of a project have been thought through at each project stage from scoping to implementation.
Identify if policy is difficult to follow; investigate why	If there are known problems following particular security policies, then an investigation into why they might be difficult to follow should be done. Ask staff about where conflicts lie between doing the job and adhering to security rules. Review the system to see if conflicts can be mitigated.
Audit delivery	Audits or assurance inspections should be conducted when appropriate to prevent shortcuts in security aspects during delivery.

Mechanisms to Develop a Communication and Education Programme and Build Security Awareness

There are many activities to include as part of a programme to build security awareness in the organisation. Other interventions in the toolkit will also inform staff about the organisation's key security messages. However, as a minimum the areas below are an excellent place to start.

HAVE AN EFFECTIVE COMMUNICATIONS PROGRAMME

Ongoing messages about security within the organisation help to keep the focus on keeping information, people and assets secure.

Mechanism	Intervention Activities
Have a communications strategy and work plan	Have a security communications strategy that outlines; 1) what you are trying to achieve by having security communications (what business objectives does it help achieve); 2) target audiences; 3) key messages; 4) media types available; and 5) an annual work plan which outlines what will be communicated and when.

Use different media	Communicate with staff using a variety of media so that the message is reaching staff in different ways. Speak to the marketing and communications team about what options you have available. Some examples include newsletters, learning lunches, emails, intranet and posters.
Have an ongoing security awareness campaign	Have an ongoing security awareness campaign with messages that tap into employees' values. For example, consider the elements of successful road safety campaigns that link values to the danger of not wearing a seatbelt or, more recently, to drink/drug driving and younger drivers.

'Road traffic today is inherently dangerous. In fact, in contrast to other modes of transport such as railways and air traffic, the road traffic system was not designed with safety as a jumping-off point. Consequently, in road traffic it is us humans who make the difference between hazard and safety, with little keeping us from harm should we make a mistake. Differently put, unlike other modes of transport that have procedures, safeguards or fallbacks to limit both the occurrence and impact of human error, road traffic relies more heavily on its users to keep accidents from occurring [– not unlike security]. Given that humans are almost inadvertently prone to make mistakes and commit violations, human behaviour is of particular interest for [both] road safety [and security] professionals' (Hoekstra and Wegman 2011; internal citation omitted).

Like road safety campaigns, security programmes should use 'behavioural' measures like the ones presented in this book (e.g. enforcement, education, training, peer pressure) as a means of influencing people to behave more securely.

Security campaigns are purposeful attempts to inform, persuade and motivate people to change their attitudes and behaviours to improve security, using specific media channels within a given period.

To recap, the example of successful road safety campaigns can inspire successful security campaigns. |
| Provide relevant communication | Ensure communication is relevant and topical, e.g. tie messages to newspaper articles, interview staff about their experiences of following a procedure that worked out for the best. |
| Develop a security communications plan to cover at least the next six months | A security communications plan is part of a security culture and awareness strategy to strategically programme what security messages will be delivered, how they will be delivered and when. See Appendix C for a sample security communications plan. |

SHARE INFORMATION ABOUT SECURITY

Keeping staff informed can help build trust and openness. Therefore, ensure that security information is widely communicated to all employees, and not just on a 'need to know' basis. This does not mean sharing *all* security information – for example, where the organisation's contingency systems are kept – but it is good for staff to know enough about security to keep them interested.

Mechanism	Intervention Activities
What security information can the organisation share?	Often security professionals make the mistake of not sharing enough information about security, but withholding information does not help build connectedness or create buy-in. Think about what and how much security information the organisation can share with its employees. For example, share recent security breaches in the news, recent changing threats or even findings from incidents. There are some global risk management surveys publically available that highlight the top risks or threats that organisations face. Use the information in these to link to the security programme.

PROVIDE STAFF TRAINING

Training is a useful activity to help staff understand the required security behaviours and to recognise security threats around them. Training and professional development are essential for the formulation of norms of expected cultural behaviour. At all levels of an organisation, managers must ensure that training is conducted to develop skills and provide tools to promote and implement security culture. Appropriate training should be provided for permanent, temporary and external or self-employed service providers.

Mechanism	Intervention Activities
Establish training needs	Identify what subjects employees should be trained in. Does the organisation require a general security training programme or is more advanced training required that looks at subjects such as security risk management? If a training programme already exists, check it is up to date and in line with the current policy and security threats.
eLearning modules	Develop an eLearning module that presents information in interesting and engaging ways. Consider how interaction can be used to make the security material more interesting.
Prioritise training participation	Participation in training should be given high priority and ensured it is not interrupted by non-urgent activities.

Training evaluation	Periodic evaluations of training programmes should be conducted and revisions incorporated as necessary.
Track and record training participation	Information on staff qualifications and participation in training should be easily accessible by the relevant authorised personnel.
No work without appropriate training	Staff should not perform work for which they lack the required skills and knowledge.
Visits by senior managers	Senior managers should periodically attend the training sessions to show their visible support.
Basic training	Basic security awareness training should instruct staff on proper workplace security as well as requirements for reporting security issues.

HAVE ENGAGING AND USEFUL WEBPAGES ON THE COMPANY INTRANET

The company intranet is usually one of the easiest communications mechanisms for delivering key messages regarding security and risk. It is a good idea to dedicate a few pages specifically to security, showing essential information to keep the organisation safe and secure. Intranet messages can inform via news pages; store soft copies of documents, including policies and procedures; communicate who the security team are and their contact details; and be used to report security breaches or near misses.

Mechanism	Intervention Activities
Link to key contacts	Introduce and list the key security personnel on the company intranet, including email addresses and phone numbers to make it easy for staff to find and contact them.
Link to key documents	Put key documents relating to security where they are easy for staff to find. If possible ensure any policies or procedures are searchable via the intranet, where available. Make sure documents are named sensibly and clearly to reflect their purpose.
Security awareness campaign information	It is useful to have some customisable areas of the webpage to include pictures, banners or text reflecting the key messages of the security awareness campaign. For example, for one month a campaign for promoting the benefit of changing passwords might run, with pictures and text used to reflect that. The next month the key message might be about disposing of confidential information correctly or challenging people entering work premises without a security pass.

Link to security awareness training	Make information about security awareness training easy to find. Is it possible to link the training to any HR Learning Management System? This might help track staff who have completed the training.
Report security issues	Make it easy for staff to report security issues, near misses or breaches. Have information about how to do this prominently displayed on the webpage.
Think about who the intranet cannot reach	Are there groups of staff who do not use the intranet or emails? For example, operational or field staff who do not use a computer. It is important to think about who will receive the messages and who will not. Think about whether different media are required to communicate with staff without computers. One suggestion is to deliver the messages with staff pay slips – people often check their payslip and they may be likely to read some other material that accompanies it.

HOW TO IMPROVE SECURITY AWARENESS

It is through security awareness initiatives that staff and contractors learn about the security requirements of their role. However, it is not enough that staff merely understand what to do; they also need to change their behaviour to help ensure that security is maintained. Security awareness is security demonstrated through behaviour.

Mechanism	Intervention Activities
Communicate importance of following procedures	Discuss why it is important to follow security policy and provide them with relevant updates if security protocols change. Disseminate this information in meetings, via newsletters, or all-staff emails.
Security awareness week	Hold a security awareness week or security awareness day to engage (or re-engage) staff. Run a security culture survey at this time to get staff thinking about security.
Utilise security awareness posters	Use posters to develop the security awareness programme. Posters are often available over the internet and are designed to help security teams promote best practice messages across any organisation as they are usually customisable.
Keep material fresh or people will not notice it after a while	If security awareness material is not kept fresh and changed regularly staff will adapt to it and, after a while, not notice it at all. Avoid the 'Hedonic adaptation' phenomenon (see section Mechanisms to Influence Senior Management Commitment and Support, above).

Mechanisms to Build Compliance and Ownership of Security Practices

Effective security culture is characterised by 'compliance with rules, regulations and procedures, and also constant vigilance and a proactive questioning attitude on the part of personnel' (IAEA 2008, 15).

THE PSYCHOLOGY OF COMPLIANCE

If people are compliant, then they behave in a way that is in accordance with a set of 'rules'. The 'rules' may be stated somewhere in a document like a policy or in a piece of legislation. Or they may be unstated, meaning they are the unwritten 'rules' or the expectations for behaviour of a group of people. The feeling that we need to comply and change our behaviour to fit in with the group, coupled with the feeling of not being able to refuse, is a strong behaviour change mechanism (Cherry n.d.[a]). This is the psychology of compliance.

Situations calling for compliance take many forms. They might include wanting staff to complete an organisational survey, undergo security awareness training (if it is not mandatory) or participate in regular risk assessments. Sometimes the request is up front and direct (what you see is what you get), while at other times it may be part of subtle and more elaborate manipulation (Kassin et al. 2011).

The factors that influence compliance

There are a number of factors that affect compliance, some of which are outlined below.

Mechanism	Intervention Activities
Common ground	Human psychology is such at we feel more connected to people that we are similar to. For example, the feeling you may experience when you find out someone went to your school, is from the country as you or worked for the same organisation as you at some stage. These are examples of having found some 'common ground' or shared experiences. When we share 'common ground' with people we feel more connected, or attracted to them and we are more likely to comply (Cherry n.d.[a]).
	On a purely business level, it could be as general as your mutual goals. For example, you may have in common the business risks you are trying to mitigate such as damage to brand and

	reputation, loss of revenue, reduced productivity, protection of customer or financial information, damage to share value, reduced regulatory compliance, reduced safety, protection of intellectual property, and protection of trade secrets.
Group affiliation	The groups we belong to, or want to belong to, can strongly influence our behaviour and make us more likely to 'go along with the crowd'. At times, we may follow the group's behaviour even when we do not believe it is the right thing to do or do not want to (Cherry n.d.[a]).
	While you may not want people to regularly go against their preferences, you might, for example, want an engineer to wear the correct PPE (even if they didn't want to), or staff to wear security passes (even if they didn't want to or feel they needed to).
Deal with larger groups rather than groups of only one or two	People are more likely to comply when more people are present. In smaller groups people feel more comfortable to speak out and give their opinions as opposed to larger groups (Cherry n.d.[a]).
Deal in groups when trying to influence difficult people	As mentioned above, a group situation makes compliance more likely. Therefore, when attempting to change an especially difficult person try to discuss issues in a group setting rather than one to one as peer pressure might persuade them to comply more readily (Cherry n.d.[a]).

Techniques to gain compliance

There are a number of techniques that can be used to gain compliance from people. These are now discussed in the table below.

Mechanism	Intervention Activities
The rule of reciprocity	This has already been discussed in this chapter under the mechanisms to manage business and organisational pressures but, to recap, people are more likely to comply if they feel that the other person has already done something for them. We have been socialised to believe that if people extend a kindness to us, then we should return the favour. Researchers have found that the reciprocity effect is so strong that it can work even when the initial favour is uninvited or comes from someone we do not like (Cherry [b]). The rule of reciprocity could be used in the following situations to elicit good security behaviours from others. For example, offer to fill in for someone or help them with a task, if they agree to lock their laptop away at the end of the day, lock their computer when not using it or some other desired security behaviour.

The 'that's not all' technique	Refer to the section on organisational systems as mechanisms to shape security culture, above.
Offer something for free in return for listening to your security message	Refer to the section on organisational systems as mechanisms to shape security culture.
The 'door-in-the-face' strategy	Refer to the section on organisational systems as mechanisms to shape security culture.
The 'foot-in-the-door' technique	In this approach, initiators start by asking for and obtaining a small commitment. Once you have already complied with the first request, you are more likely also to comply with a second, larger request. For example, your co-worker asks if you could help write a paper for the board but after agreeing, he then asks if you could just continue to write the rest of the paper and finish it off (Cherry n.d.[b]). In relation to building a security culture, you may be able to get a manager to agree to a security review of their area involving a limited scope. Once that is agreed, you may be able to widen the scope if it made sense to consider other related areas that impact each other.
Ingratiation	Gaining approval from a person, or ingratiating yourself, helps to get on the right side of them which can help secure their compliance (Cherry n.d.[a]). In a security context, you might try to persuade an executive to wear their security pass consistently by flattering them and saying that it is what effective leaders like themselves would naturally do.

INVOLVE STAFF TO BUILD OWNERSHIP

Effective security culture depends on teamwork and cooperation among all staff, not just the security team. Therefore, it makes sense to involve staff in security so that they have more personal ownership for security practices.

Ensure that staff know what their role is in relation to security

Staff should understand what they can personally do to maintain security, that security is not something just done by the security team, but by everybody in the organisation.

Mechanism	Intervention Activities
Include in role descriptions	Managers are responsible for ensuring that there is a clear understanding within the organisation of the security roles and responsibilities of each individual, including clarity concerning levels of authority and lines of communication. In practice, this can be facilitated by including in job descriptions how staff can help meet the organisation's security goals.
Align business objectives with security objectives	There should be a clear line of sight between the organisation's business plan and objectives and the security team's plan and objectives. The security team exists to support the business, so this needs to be clearly demonstrated to foster ownership.
Communicate the policy in ways that are personal to people	Communicate the security policy in a manner that is meaningful for staff. Justify procedures in ways that relate to people's day-to-day jobs so that they understand why procedures exist.

How to give staff influence over the way security is handled

Improving the amount of influence staff have on the way security is handled in teams will increase their buy-in and compliance with security matters. It also pays to design security with the people in mind.

Mechanism	Intervention Activities
Involve staff in decisions and the design of procedures	Involve and consult with staff in decisions about security that affect them so that they feel like their input has been valued.
Set up a security committee	Set up a security committee with representatives from across the business to input into security matters. This way security becomes something that is owned by the business, not just the security team.
Use security surveys to get feedback from staff	Use a security survey to ask the business for feedback on security issues. These could be added to the end of a security culture survey to inform the business about topical matters.
Security suggestion scheme	Set up a security suggestion scheme to get ideas for how security can be improved within the business.
Engage employees in security strategy and priorities	Discuss with staff strategies and priorities for security. Update them on the security risks that are relevant to them and work on mitigation plans together.

ORGANISATIONAL OWNERSHIP AND INTERNALISATION OF CULTURE

For a security culture to form, staff need common security attitudes and practices. This next section is about generating organisational ownership for security and the internalisation of security culture.

Foster group awareness of security issues

Humans are social creatures and we enjoy feeling part of a group. Most of our behaviour is conducted in the company of others – most of what we do has a social context (real or imagined) to it (Earls 2009). Therefore, get staff to interact in group settings to help spread security awareness throughout the organisation.

Mechanism	Intervention Activities
Position security material in group settings	Observe and think about how people interact in the organisation. Place security awareness materials in places where people gather to foster group awareness.
Run awareness training in group settings	If possible, run security awareness training in group settings so that the subject can be normalised.
Use 'social influencers' to spread the word	'Social influencers' are those people who shape the opinions and behaviours of their peers (Earls 2009). They have a natural ability to persuade people in their peer group or network of their views. Seek them out in your organisation and then ask them to spread the word about security.
Use 'super connectors' to spread the word	Another type of influencer to get on your side are 'super connectors'. These are people who have an incredible ability to connect with anyone and everyone (Earls 2009). These people are useful because they know everyone and so can carry your message to all areas of the organisation.
Hold a security awareness week	Security awareness weeks have already been discussed in the section describing the mechanisms to develop a communication and education programme and build security awareness (above), but these are also an excellent way to harness the power of the group and get people talking about security.

Reduce harmful counter-cultures and sub-cultures

Counter-cultures are those negative patterns of behaviour within an organisation that run against management intentions. For example, there may be a culture of the rules not applying to contractors in the business or a certain area of the business refusing to clear their desks and lock away laptops.

Mechanism	Intervention Activities
The rules apply to everyone	Communicate the fact that security policies and rules apply to everyone.
Enforce the fact that the rules apply to everyone	Once it has been communicated that the security policies and rules apply to everyone, discipline those who do not follow policy and reward those who do.
Encourage peer pressure	It has already been mentioned that humans are social beings, so encourage colleagues to 'lean on' those who do not follow policy. Peer pressure is a powerful motivator.
Encourage people to do what is right	Appeal to people's desire to do what is fair and right. Encourage them to follow policy, just as others do, because it is the right thing to do.
Check levels of compliance	People are more likely to follow security measures if they know someone will check up on them. So check levels of compliance through audits.

How to reduce insider threat

'An insider is a person who exploits, or has the intention to exploit, their legitimate access to an organisation's assets for unauthorised purposes. This can be a permanent, temporary, seconded, contract or agency worker. … Some of the more common insider acts include: unauthorised disclosure of information, process corruption (where an employee has illegitimately altered an internal process for their own ends), corporate espionage and theft.' (CPNI 2014, 3)

Mechanism	Intervention Activities
Raise awareness of the insider threat	The insider threat is often only discussed once when there is a high-profile example of it in the media. However, it is important to ensure that both management and staff know what it is and how it can be mitigated.

Consider how to deal with an insider threat breach	Responding to an insider threat security breach requires coordination between managers, HR and the security team. Find appropriate training for these groups so that the situation can be dealt with effectively from a legal and forensic viewpoint (CPNI March 2011).
Monitoring systems in place	Ensure the organisation has monitoring systems in place to identify unauthorised activity and access to systems (CPNI 2014).
Pre-employment screening	Reduce vulnerability to insider threat through pre-employment screening. A documented screening process should match the risks and threats associated with specific work roles and responsibilities. This should go beyond simple reference checks, and needs to include identity verification, criminal record checks and financial checks (CPNI 2014).
Employ risk-based continuous monitoring of staff with security clearance	Another recommendation to mitigate insider threat is to, in effect, continuously monitor the activities and behaviours of those with security clearance. In the past, once an individual received security clearance, it was not reviewed for another five or ten years. Continuous security vetting should employ a risk management approach and be based on the sensitivity and amount of information individuals have access to.
Train managers to identify unusual behaviour	Work with managers to help them identify unusual behaviour early and intervene (CPNI 2014).

MONITORING AND ASSURANCE

This section discusses how to ensure that an appropriate amount of monitoring and assurance is in place.

How to provide assurance that security procedures are followed

Assurance provides verification that security policies are being followed.

Mechanism	Intervention Activities
Have reporting mechanisms in place	Have reporting mechanisms in place that allow staff to report security issues. Consider whether a confidential reporting system is necessary.
Reward reporting of security issues	Reward those who report security issues to encourage that behaviour. Effective performance leading to better security should also be rewarded.

Performance measurement	Ensure the organisation uses benchmarks and targets to understand, achieve and improve performance at all levels.
Compare against targets and communicate to staff	Performance results should be compared with the targets and regularly communicated to staff.
Take action on poor performance	Ensure that action is taken when security performance does not fully match the goals.
Automate reporting	Automate reporting where possible to streamline the process. Consider how dashboard reporting could be used to present relevant security performance to managers.
Timely mitigation of breaches	Ensure that any action, mitigation or follow-up related to the reporting of security breaches is completed in a timely manner, and reasons why they are not.

Have relevant recording/monitoring systems

Improving security culture requires persistent effort and frequent monitoring to discourage inappropriate behaviours.

Mechanism	Intervention Activities
Review monitoring systems regularly	It is not enough to have monitoring in place; the results of such should be reviewed to verify compliance.
Disclose the monitoring of employees to staff	Where appropriate, keep all staff regularly informed of any monitoring taking place throughout the organisation to discourage breaches of security. However, be careful not to reveal vulnerabilities. Some organisations may not wish to reveal their monitoring capability or lack because of that.
Communicate the outcomes of monitoring	Inform personnel of the outcomes of any monitoring so that it discourages inappropriate behaviour.
Provide constructive feedback based on monitoring outcomes	Managers have the responsibility to ensure that appropriate behaviour is reinforced through constructive feedback.
Inform staff that they will be monitored in the IT policy	Ensure that the IT policy states that employees will be monitored, and make sure staff read and understand the policy.

Conduct regular risk assessments

Risk assessments are critical in the security space to ensure that the organisation understands what it needs to protect and to ensure appropriate mitigations are in place that match the threats. Risk assessments will also help prioritise resources to treat risks.

Mechanism	Intervention Activities
Review threats and risks annually	Hold an annual risk identification and risk assessment session with subject experts to ensure the organisation understands what its threats are.
Encourage staff to identify threats and risks	Ensure staff know how to raise security risks and where to get help and advice if required.
Develop SMART mitigation plans to address threats and risks	Ensure that action plans to mitigate risks are SMART (Specific, Measurable, Achievable, Realistic and Timely).

Have appropriate access control and classification

Controlling access to sensitive information is a vital part of the security function. Accordingly, the organisation must implement classification and control measures for protecting sensitive information and ensure that access (to sites, buildings, information etc.) is controlled adequately.

Mechanism	Intervention Activities
Document classification and control	Ensure that classification and control requirements are clearly documented and well understood by staff.
Classification processes and protocols	Ensure that clear and effective processes and protocols exist for classifying and handling information both inside and outside the organisation.
Segregate sensitive information	Classified information should be segregated and securely stored and managed.
Staff understand the importance of classification and access measures	Ensure that staff are aware of and understand the importance of adhering to the controls on information.
Security passes	Ensure that staff visibly wear security passes.
Maintain cyber systems	Cyber systems should be maintained to ensure that they are secure; accredited by an appropriate authority; and operated in accordance with procedures.
Train staff to deal with suspicious behaviour	Ensure that staff know how to deal with suspicious behaviour as part of the training for security personnel on how to recognise and deal appropriately with suspicious incidents.

Summary

An organisation can use many mechanisms to shape security culture, and the next chapter provides the steps to follow.

References

Adler, Paul, Charles Heckscher and Laurence Prusak. 2011. Building a collaborative enterprise. *Harvard Business Review* 89(7–8), 94–101.

AGCareers. 2009. *Delegating Effectively*. Accessed May 20, 2015. http://www.agcareers.com/newsletters/delegating.htm.

Aguirre, DeAnne, Louisa Finn and Ashley Harshak. 2007. Ready, willing, and engaged: A practical guide for sponsors of change. *Strategy&*. Accessed April 22, 2015. http://www.strategyand.pwc.com/media/uploads/READYWILLINGANDENGAGED.pdf.

Bagshaw, Mike. n.d. *Building Stress Immunity*. Active Trainer. Accessed May 20, 2015. http://www.fenman.co.uk/traineractive/training-activity/Managing-pressure-positively.html.

Berry, Leonard L., Ann M. Mirabito and William B. Baun. 2010. What's the hard return on employee wellness programs? *Harvard Business Review* (December). Accessed May 20, 2015. https://hbr.org/2010/12/whats-the-hard-return-on-employee-wellness-programs.

Butler, Ken. 2012. *Are You Happy at Work?* March 12. Accessed April 2015, 21. https://areyouhappyatwork.wordpress.com/2012/03/12/avoid-the-blame-game/.

CESG. 2009. *HMG IA Standard No. 1: Technical Risk Assessment*. UK Cabinet Office National Technical Authority for Information Assurance. October. Accessed May 6, 2015. www.cesg.gov.uk/publications/documents/is1_risk_assessment.pdf.

Cherry, Kendra. n.d. [a]. What is compliance? *About Education*. Accessed April 22, 2015. http://psychology.about.com/od/socialinfluence/a/compliance.htm.

———. n.d. [b]. What is the rule of reciprocity? *About Education*. Accessed April 22, 2015. http://psychology.about.com/od/socialinfluence/f/rule-of-reciprocity.htm.

CPNI. 2011. *Investigating Employees of Concern: A Good Practice Guide*. Centre for the Protection of National Infrastructure. March. Accessed May 24, 2015. http://www.cpni.gov.uk/documents/publications/2011/2011004-persec-investigating_employees_of_concern.pdf?epslanguage=en-gb.

———. 2014. *Ongoing Personal Security: A Good Practice Guide*. Centre for the Protection of National Infrastructure. April. Accessed May 24, 2015. http://www.cpni.gov.uk/documents/publications/2014/2014006-ongoing-personal-security.pdf?epslanguage=en-gb.

Earls, Mark. 2009. *Herd: How to Change Mass Behaviour by Harnessing Our True Nature*. Chichester: Wiley.

Feloni, Richard. 2014. Richard Branson's 4 rules for making difficult decisions. *Business Insider Australia*, October 9. Accessed May 20, 2015. http://www.businessinsider.com.au/how-richard-branson-makes-decisions-2014-10.

Goffee, Robert and Gareth Jones. 2000. Why should anyone be led by you? *Harvard Business Review*. September–October. Accessed May 10, 2015. https://hbr.org/2000/09/why-should-anyone-be-led-by-you.

Goleman, Daniel. 2000. Leadership that gets results. *Harvard Business Review* March–April, 78–90.

Harshak, Ashley, DeAnne Aguirre and Anna Brown. 2010. Making change happen and making it stick: Delivering sustainable organizational change. *Strategy&: Formerly Booz & Company*. Accessed April 22, 2015. http://www.strategyand.pwc.com/media/file/Strategyand_Making-change-happen-and-making-it-stick.pdf.

Hoekstra, Tamara and Fred Wegman. 2011. Improving the effectiveness of road safety campaigns: Current and new practices. *IATSS Research* 34(2), 80–86.

HRZone. n.d. *What are Tangible Rewards*. Accessed May 18, 2015. http://www.hrzone.com/hr-glossary/what-are-tangible-rewards.

IAEA. 2008. *Nuclear Security Culture: Implementing Guide*. International Atomic Energy Agency. Accessed April 22, 2015. http://www-pub.iaea.org/MTCD/Publications/PDF/Pub1347_web.pdf.

Kassin, Saul, Steven Fein and Hazel Rose Markus. 2011. *Social Psychology*. Belmont, CA: Wadsworth, Cengage Learning.

Lyubomirsky, Sonja. 2013. *The Myths of Happiness: What Should Make You Happy, but Doesn't, What Shouldn't Make You Happy, but Does*. London: Penguin.

meQuilibrium. 2015. Stress tip: Be willing to listen. *Huffington Post*. December 2. Accessed April 21, 2015. http://www.huffingtonpost.com/2015/02/12/mequilibrium-stress-tip_n_6664096.html.

National Counter Terrorism Security Office. 2014. *Guidance: Protecting Your Business's Assets*. November 24. Accessed April 21, 2015. hhtps://www.gov.uk/protecting-your-business-assets.

NHS. 2014. *Why Sitting Too Much is Bad for Your Health*. October 14. Accessed May 20, 2015. http://www.nhs.uk/livewell/fitness/pages/sitting-and-sedentary-behaviour-are-bad-for-your-health.aspx.

Petersen, Lars Birkholm. 2012. *Best Practices for Developing Personas with the Sitecore Customer Engagement Platform*. Sitecore/VLM. Accessed April 22, 2015. file:///C:/Users/Tom&Hills/Downloads/whitepaper_best%20practices%20developing%20personas_sitecorecep%20(1).pdf.

Ramachandran, V.S. 2012. Do mirror neurons give us empathy? *Greater Good: The Science of a Meaningful Life*. March 29. Accessed March 13, 2015. http://greatergood.berkeley.edu/article/item/do_mirror_neurons_give_empathy.

Root, George N. III. n.d. What are the employees' responsibilities to maintain a security policy? *Chron*. Accessed May 20, 2015. http://smallbusiness.chron.com/employees-responsibilities-maintain-security-policy-12087.html.

Sensenig, Kevin J. 2009. Human potential untangled. *HRZone*. May 29. Accessed May 20, 2015. http://www.dalecarnegie.cz/assets/1/7/Successful_Engagement_-_Human_Potential_Untangled.pdf.

Strohmetz, David. 2002. Sweetening the till: The use of candy to increase restaurant tipping. *Journal of Applied Social Psychology* 32, 300–309.

Williams, Terry. 2012. *The Brain-Based Boss: Adding Serious Value through Employee Engagement*. Wellington: Thomson Reuters.

Chapter 6

How to Prioritise
What to Do Next

The purpose of this chapter is to:

- Describe the steps for security culture change.

- Provide advice about choosing or prioritising initiatives from the toolkit in Chapter 5.

- Outline how to set up incremental change and manage the security budget with respect to change initiatives.

- Provide an overview of how to manage different cultures and silo behaviour in the organisation.

There are many things an organisation can do to improve its security culture, but how should it prioritise initiatives to best effect? This is the topic of this chapter. It looks at general organisational and culture change principles and steps. It then discusses how to choose and prioritise the security culture change initiatives described in Chapter 5. The big issue of budget is further explored to review what can be done for little or no money, and how to manage 'silos' in the organisation is discussed.

The early chapters discussed the basic concepts of security culture and managing people risk and their measurement, while Chapter 5 provided an armoury of security culture change initiatives to improve attitudes to security within the business. But how should one decide which initiatives to use? The key to this lies in the assessment of the security culture: identify the current type of security culture and then decide what type is needed to achieve the business objectives. This way it is possible to design a road map of how to get there.

Steps for Shaping Security Culture

The steps for shaping culture are now outlined using the Competence Assurance Solutions (CAS) culture change processes (Luther and Johnson 2008).

1. EVALUATE THE EXISTING SECURITY CULTURE (CURRENT SECURITY CULTURE)

The first place to start is to determine the current company culture in relation to security. What type of security culture is currently operating in the business? Do people view security positively or negatively? Do they follow security policies and rules even when their supervisor is not looking? And so on.

Multiple perspectives should be incorporated into the process to create greater accuracy. This should not just be an activity of the security group. Ideally, the entire organisation would be surveyed – preferably using more than one method of assessment – to obtain the most accurate and representative picture of the existing security culture.

Chapter 5 outlines assessment checklists and tools which can be used with other methods such as interviews, surveys, questionnaires, conversations with staff, teaming up employees from different parts of the company, or meeting with all employees one-on-one and discussing the company culture. Alternatively, hiring a consultant is another option to get an objective perspective.

2. DECIDE ON THE TYPE OF ORGANISATION WANTED (TARGET SECURITY CULTURE)

Once there is an understanding of the current security culture, the next step is to determine the qualities to instil in the company culture, based on the company's vision. For instance, some organisations might prioritise values such as innovation, professionalism, accountability or respect for others. These might be considered the characteristics of excellence and can differ between organisations. However, the profile of the target security culture should be based on the same factors that are used to evaluate the existing (current) culture. It is best to include the senior management and executives in discussions about the aspirational security culture as they are responsible for driving company strategy and without their support little will change.

Reorientation of organisational culture is only possible if there are compelling reasons and a shared understanding of the need for change among managers and employees. The foremost goal of cultural change is to sensitise every employee to the necessity of conscious handling of corporate risk and security.

3. IDENTIFY THE 'LEVERS' TO PULL TO EMBED THE DESIRED SECURITY CULTURE WITHIN THE ORGANISATION

Again, Chapter 5 outlines the mechanisms or levers the organisation controls that can help create the right attitudes and behaviours required to fulfil the target culture. Determine which ones are useful in the context of your organisation.

4. CREATE A PLAN TO ENSURE THE MECHANISMS ARE APPLIED CONSISTENTLY AND APPROPRIATELY

Formulate an actionable plan to realise the new cultural vision. The mechanisms chosen now need to be applied consistently to effect change. Senior management is responsible for implementing and monitoring this plan, hence the importance of this culture change being led from the top.

> Securing 'buy in' from employees is crucial to the success of the action plan. They must know their input was instrumental in creating new policies and that their continued involvement is essential. Transparency and communication are key to making this happen. All employees must understand that they each have a continuing role to play. Management should reward risk-sensitive behaviour that helps build the target culture and dissuades unethical and insecure behavior. (Bungartz 2010)

5. REVIEW PROGRESS AND EFFECTIVENESS OF APPROACH

Re-evaluate the company's security culture at least annually or as conditions change. Managers often fail to take a hard look at how their company serves them in a changing market – a definite mistake. For example, consider how changing the organisation's structure or adding new employees may also have changed the security culture.

Choosing or Prioritising Initiatives from the Toolkit in Chapter 5

The assessment of how well the different mechanisms are operating will guide the prioritisation of culture change initiatives. Each mechanism is a way of changing attitudes, behaviour and, ultimately the culture, of an organisation.

Therefore, one could look to utilise all the mechanisms to effect change; but with so many, some prioritisation is useful to determine what to do first. In addition, often issues of budget will prohibit what and how much can be done.

While all the mechanisms and initiatives outlined in Chapter 5 are useful to effect change, not all of them will suit all organisations. Therefore, due consideration needs to be given to the existing and desired organisational culture and what will and will not work in that context. For example, if the desired culture is process oriented – where focus on compliance and quality of output is important – then this culture should encompass incident analysis and continuous improvement; professionalism and responsibility acceptance as well as formal feedback and reward and discipline to aid motivation towards security issues. Employees would then have a clearer indication of the good and bad security behaviours relevant to the organisation. Addressing those issues and reviewing the consistent application of security across the business would heighten the importance of its security.

Conversely, in a process-oriented security culture, while not unbeneficial, it would not be as effective to focus on mechanisms that give staff greater involvement or empowerment. The very nature of the culture is to avoid employees designing their own security procedures, and they would also not be left to take care of security in their own areas of work without the outcomes being monitored.

If, however an organisation is seeking a participative culture it would encourage greater staff involvement in security issues. It would be important for that organisation to involve and consult staff on security matters to ensure buy-in. However, the final decision would likely rest with the management.

A culture of staff participation is likely to lead to less consistency, resulting in a need for greater flexibility in the application of security rules. In this case, focusing on whether security practices are applied consistently throughout the entire business and enforcing security measures would be less useful for developing the culture. Therefore, mechanisms and initiatives should not be blindly applied. Some thought about what is appropriate for the organisation's unique culture is required. This is why consultants are often used for culture change projects. However, some due diligence to sense check the action plan prior to implementation is all that is required.

Start with the weakest areas first and work from those mechanisms that have been identified through assessments, interviews and/or focus groups. For example, if it was identified that there is negative feedback and poor scoring on aspects of management support and commitment that are crucial to the desired type of security culture, then these will be key areas to focus on to improve the situation.

Change Management Tips and Budget Considerations

HOW DISRUPTIVE IS THE SECURITY CULTURE CHANGE?

The size of a change will impact how employees feel about it and their reaction – positive or negative – to it. Employees, and people in general, are likely to react more positively to a change which does not move them too far from where they are – an incremental change. If the change is large, even radical, they are likely to react very differently. This in turn will affect how a change should be managed. When thinking about developing or changing the security culture, ask the following questions:

- How big is the gap between the current and the desired security culture?

- How different is the current state from the desired state?

These may seem simple questions, but it is important to understand just how much change or disruption is taking place because it impacts how we will manage that change. The answers to these questions provide an invaluable starting point when developing the right security culture change management approach.

With small security culture change less senior-level sponsorship may be required; different and less involved communication plans may be needed; and less management training and coaching is involved. With large change, often called the big bang effect, the change happens on a certain date and a new system is adopted all at once. This is a riskier approach than incremental change as there are fewer learning opportunities incorporated along the way. In other words, small changes require small amounts of change management and large changes require large amounts of change management. Applying a 'one-size-fits all' approach is not appropriate.

The same change project will also impact different types of employees differently, so it is useful to scale and customise the change management depending on the target audience. To improve the change management success, it can be better to work with some of the existing organisational structures and processes, rather than change everything.

ESTABLISHING QUICK WINS

Quick wins are essentially what it says on the tin – the most obvious opportunities that are readily achievable and do not require a lot of effort. Quick wins are particularly important for new leaders as, apart from improving their performance, there can be business ramifications of not getting off to a quick start. A quick win allows managers to show they can get the business where it needs to be in a short time – which is imperative in the current economic climate. Quick wins are also critical for projects with long time frames as it allows the achievement of some quick results early on, helping to establish credibility inside the organisation and giving the political capital needed to succeed in the long run. Culture change takes time and therefore is a good example of a long-term project. A quick win may also buy the luxury of time in case more difficult challenges arise.

So it is established that quick wins are essential and that a results orientation is important for culture change success. However, results should not cause conflict with others' individual goals; otherwise efforts could negatively impact teamwork and dynamics. It is important not to leave a trail of people who are 'disengaged, no longer feeling a part of the work, not motivated and not making contributions to [the] priorities' of the change (Melymuka 2009). That would be counterproductive to the fundamentals of this book, which is about how to motivate behaviour and create positive attitudes to security.

It should also be remembered that success does not have to come as a result of one person's expertise; it could be a team effort. This will give longer-lasting performance as everyone is able to share in and is engaged with the win. It is not just about results; it is also about working with others and building talent. This could be called fostering a collective quick win.

BUDGET CONSIDERATIONS

This section is about how to get 'the biggest bang for your buck' when undertaking a security culture change project. Developing and managing a business's security culture is not about purchasing and implementing multiple solutions. It is about identifying the solutions needed and ensuring that they 'cover off' the business risk identified through the assessment of the desired security culture state.

TAKE A BUSINESS-CENTRIC FOCUS AND PARTNER WITH OTHER GROUPS

This requires not just focusing on the operational security controls required, but also involves a business-centric undertaking covering activities such as risk assessments, asset valuation (including people, information and physical assets) and process optimisation.

Where possible, it is important to partner with the business on improvements and changes made so that investments in security are effective, efficient and sustainable, and support the business goals – in other words they are not a waste of money and effort. Key groups/departments to partner with – apart from the obvious physical security and information security – are legal, compliance, human resources (HR), communications and marketing, and privacy. These groups frequently have mutual interests and objectives and may be amenable to sharing or providing additional resources, such as funding or distribution. To obtain the support of these groups incorporate their needs into the security culture change programme. There may be certain security awareness messages which can be included from the partner groups; for example it would be easy to include some legal and compliance content.

The security initiatives to invest in are the ones that build resiliency and provide balanced coverage of preventative, detective and responsive controls. They should also cover people, processes and technology, and ensure that these factors are not out of balance.

ENLIST SENIOR LEVEL SUPPORT AND COMMITMENT

The support and commitment of senior management has already been discussed as an important part of building a security culture in organisations – that is, security programmes with senior level support are more likely to be successful. There is a powerful motivational and behaviour change force which is harnessed in this case. Senior level support also tends to provide more freedom to the culture change project, a larger budget and support from other groups. This should therefore be focused on first, before doing anything else. The interventions toolkit in Chapter 5 lists a number of activities to secure the senior support and commitment required.

DO IT IN-HOUSE IF POSSIBLE

Not all initiatives require a significant investment from the organisation and many initiatives can be done in-house a lot cheaper. While a large budget helps, and outsourcing to other professionals removes some of the burden from security staff, organisations can do a lot on their own for little or no money. Creativity is not always a requirement, but there are a lot of creative ideas in Chapter 5 to pick and choose from. For example, it costs nothing (except time) to create a briefing pack for managers to discuss security with their teams; or to carry out regular desk sweeps and send a letter to anyone found to have left sensitive material unsecured on their desk or in an unlocked cupboard.

ENSURE THE BUDGET IS BUILT INTO THE CORPORATE PLANNING ROUND

It is difficult to run a security culture change programme without a budget for it. Therefore, ensure that the change programme and its initiatives are included in the security budget and plan. The key message here is that it can take time for a business plan and strategy to be accepted, so it is important to aim several months ahead and start early. This means being organised and prepared prior to budgeting time. Solicit the support of management, assess the current state of the security culture and consider the desired state. Identify those mechanisms required to change the security culture in the desired direction; prioritise which initiatives to implement; and ensure those initiatives are included in the next security budget. The budget required is then justified by the link between the desired state, the mechanisms required to change it and the initiatives chosen to do so.

Managing Different Cultures and Silo Behaviour in the Organisation

WHAT TO DO WITH DIFFERENT CULTURES

It is possible for different or opposing security cultures to exist within one company. This can result in 'silos' of behaviour where one group, team or department exhibits a different set of behaviours from another. Measuring the culture and filtering information by factors such as group or location are good ways to identify and locate any differences.

WHAT RISKS DO DIFFERENT CULTURES POSE TO AN ORGANISATION? THE SILO MENTALITY

'Silos' can occur in all types of organisations whether large or small. Whenever silo behaviour does occur, it is detrimental to an organisation's ability to succeed in a rapidly changing world (Kotter 2011). For example, if one group in an organisation works hard to protect customer information but a privacy breach occurs in another group that does not, the impact of that breach will affect the reputation of all groups equally.

'It's also important to note that silos can be vertical or horizontal. Individual units can have high barriers between them or senior leadership can be completely isolated from lower management levels' (Kotter 2011). The existence of silos may also mean that senior leaders disagree over the current or desired security culture states and where the organisation needs to head. In this case, breaking down silos by being able to describe the current and desired security culture will help gain collective agreement on the organisation's direction in terms of its security and risk profile.

The consequences of silos are distrust, poor communication and complacency; they also inhibit the ability to respond quickly to threats in the environment or seize opportunities (Kotter 2011). A security culture programme can break down silos, through being targeted at these problem areas and including people from across the business.

Summary

This chapter outlined the steps needed for security culture change and gave guidance on how to choose and prioritise initiatives from the intervention toolkit (Chapter 5) for an action plan. It indicated that the size of the security culture change will impact how the change programme is managed, and discussed security budget, in particular how to justify the budget and how some in-house initiatives can help stretch a modest budget. The chapter finished by providing an overview of how to manage different cultures and silo behaviour by reducing the consequences of silo behaviour and including representatives from across the organisation in the security culture change programme group. The next chapter will look at how to measure the impact of a security culture change programme through the use of metrics.

References

Bungartz, Oliver. 2010. Talking points – Creating enterprise: Wide risk awareness are your clients building prudent 'risk cultures'? *RSM International*. Accessed May 26, 2015. http://rsmi.com/publications/talking-points/443-creating-enterprise-wide-risk-awareness-are-your-clients-building-prudent-%E2%80%98risk-cultures%E2%80%99.html.

Kotter, John. 2011. Breaking down silos: A Q&A with John Kotter. *Life Science Leader*, May 12. Accessed May 25, 2015. http://www.lifescienceleader.com/doc/breaking-down-silos-a-q-a-with-john-kotter-0001.

Luther, R.E. and C.E. Johnson. 2008. *Culture Management in the UK Rail Industry*. 3rd IET International Conference on System Safety, Birmingham, October 20–22.

Melymuka, Kathleen. 2009. How new leaders can achieve quick wins. *CIO.com*, January 26. Accessed May 25, 2015. http://www.cio.com/article/2431129/careers-staffing/how-new-leaders-can-achieve-quick-wins.html.

Chapter 7

Metrics: Measuring the Impact on the Organisation

The purpose of this chapter is to:

- Discuss the importance of using metrics.

- Provide techniques for identifying security culture programme impact.

- Discuss the real financial cost of security breaches.

- Provide techniques for presenting metrics to senior managers and staff.

- Suggest longer-term considerations to keep security culture strong.

Security metrics is a vast topic, but an important one to consider in tracking the performance of a security programme. Without performance metrics the measurement of outcomes, intervention change and return on investment against the business case cannot be substantiated.

This chapter will discuss security metrics generally, as well as metrics specifically for security culture and people risk management. This is because it is possible to apply the same principles to all security domains: culture, physical security, information security, personnel security or business continuity and disaster recovery.

This chapter outlines techniques to identify security metrics, particularly those around security culture, people risk management and awareness programme effectiveness. It will help ascertain whether security has improved or whether the money spent was just a gimmick. It also outlines how often security culture and people risk should be monitored; how to present metrics to senior management and staff in a digestible and meaningful way; and how to keep security culture strong and people risk low over the longer term. The resources include two examples of security culture, people risk and awareness dashboards, and a programme status report.

The Importance of Using Metrics

One of the key factors in having any successful programme is being able to prove that the initiative made a positive difference. The only way to do this is to collect information and develop metrics before starting the security culture change and awareness efforts, and then measure these during and after the initiative, to demonstrate improvements or not. Without a baseline it is hard to demonstrate that the initiative had more than assumed success. It is also difficult to manage any activity that cannot be measured, so metrics provide aspects of good governance. A main function of metrics, measuring and monitoring is to support decisions. For metrics to be useful, the information they provide must be relevant to the recipient so that informed decisions can be made.

Good governance relies on assessment of the adequacy of what is being measured, in this case security culture and people risk management. Governance might concern the measurement of a work programme (for example an overall security programme, a security culture programme, a security awareness programme, an information security programme and so on). It should also have a bearing on how good security is and whether the security spending is justified. Alternatively, it is possible to track progress towards fixed objectives to be achieved.

The key is to adopt a pragmatic and useful approach to monitoring the effectiveness of security. It should be relevant to the audience; allow the overall programme to be adjusted accordingly based on results; and help decisions on future investments (Volchkov 2013).

The audience for metrics is most likely to be senior management, but metrics may also be useful to other levels of management and staff in general. For example, following a security survey it is essential that staff are informed of the results, otherwise they may view responding to surveys as a waste of time if their outcomes and resulting actions are not communicated. Just about every group in a company has to prove their value, and security should not expect to be an exception.

WHY IT IS DIFFICULT TO MEASURE SECURITY

Standard security measures such as recording the number and types of incidents are indicative of aspects of security, but they fail to provide any actual information about how secure an organisation is. Merely observing incidents or studying statistics does not enable us to reach conclusions about the adequacy of security. For example, how many incidents are allowed in a good security set-up? If a culture of reporting has just been embedded then the number of incidents is likely to go up – what implications does that have? What happens if there are no incidents?

There are equations that can be used to establish security factors such as annual loss expectancy (ALE) or total cost of ownership (TCO), but these equations rely on estimates of a loss and its likelihood of occurrence – information that is not easy to estimate, or come by (Volchkov 2013). In addition, organisations do not typically share information, data or statistics on vulnerabilities and incidents because of the negative impact this could have on customers, shareholders and the general public. There are also no common definitions of breach, incident, attack, loss or investment (Volchkov 2013). They mean different things to different people and different organisations.

During the sales process, IT solution providers often talk of their ability to reduce costs based on their model for calculating return on investment (ROI). However, each solution does not usually cover only one risk. Organisations want flexible, holistic solutions that will cover a range of risks. So, apart from it being extremely difficult to assign a solution to each specific risk, there are also positive and negative effects to each risk factor, not to mention the supplementary costs associated with maintenance (Volchkov 2013). These factors, along with the constant evolution of threats, makes measurement based on a programme of individual IT components difficult.

Compliance with a standard does not necessarily mean good security either. Standards and frameworks can be used to assess a security posture; however, they do not provide evaluation criteria and presuppose the existence of processes that not all organisations will have (Volchkov 2013). They also do not generally recommend how to measure security. The alignment of metrics to standards will be discussed further in the following section on measurement techniques.

GOOD NEWS AND BAD NEWS ON MEASURING IMPACT

All is not lost however. The good news is that management are not generally interested in technical/operational metrics or return on investment of a particular isolated security component (Volchkov 2013). They are interested in the efficiency of a work programme or the countermeasures in place. These are the commercial aspects of the programme: for example the revenue generated; the costs saved; the improvement of services or products; and the control of spending.

Metrics therefore need to adopt this sort of approach and language to be meaningful. This includes covering 'functional and strategic alignment; security performance objectives; compliance management; security team performance; and security added value for customers' (Volchkov 2013).

The strategy for investment in security has to target the high-risk areas and the improvement of less adequate or immature processes (Volchkov 2013). In order to target these areas, they need to be measured. In relation to metrics, advice, lessons and examples are generally available in books, articles and papers. But one of the difficulties of metrics is that applying them to a particular organisation requires thinking about the unique context of that organisation.

Fortunately, however, measurements of those intangible aspects of security, such as culture, only need to be good 'enough' and certain 'enough'. No matter how fuzzy the measurement, it is still a measurement if it tells more than was known before and allows sound business decisions to be made (Hubbard 2010).

Metrics only need to provide enough certainty and clarity to help decide. The challenge is to determine what 'enough' is for a particular decision. After all, in life many major and risky decisions are made without all the information; they are also made with minimal amounts of proper risk analysis (Hubbard 2010).

The job of security is to reduce risks to acceptable levels, at acceptable costs. But what is an acceptable level of risk? Is it practicable? What is an acceptable cost to achieve it? These are not just decisions for the security group, but business decisions which must be made by the management team. Thus it is the role of security and risk management practitioners to enable senior and middle management to make effective risk decisions by providing them with the parts of the risk picture that relate to their decisions, with some 'before and after' comparisons (Hubbard 2010).

Another way to show the impact of a programme is through ongoing discussions with senior management about the real dollar cost of security breaches. This was discussed in detail in Chapter 3, but the distillation of that information is that only 20 per cent of the cost of IT security breaches is from lost revenue due to system unavailability (Ponemon Institute 2013). The bulk – the remaining 80 per cent – is other business costs such as reputation and brand damage, lost productivity, compliance and regulatory costs and IT costs.

In order to continue these conversations with management and keep risks at the front of the mind, when a breach occurs in other organisations and hits the news it is a good idea to point out to the management that it did not happen to their organisation. The conversation is then about whether this is because the right risk mitigation mechanisms are in place, or just luck. Either way, it then becomes easier to relate that breaches can and do happen every day. This will be particularly relevant for organisations in the same industry as yours. That said, cyber threats in particular are not personal. A hacker's software is unlikely to target your organisation for any other reason than it is just looking for vulnerabilities, open doors, online.

Techniques for Measuring Programme Impact

We have established that there are numerous security metrics that can be collected. These include, but are not limited to:

- audit results
- results of surveys, particularly year on year which enable comparison
- the results of desk sweeps and other assurance and 'checking' activities
- alignment against standards and frameworks, e.g. ISO 27000 series, Control Objectives for Information and Related Technology (COBIT) or National Institute of Standards and Technology (NIST)
- compliance survey metrics
- the number of security breaches reported/incidents per month
- near misses reported per month
- estimated cost in human hours of incidents and/or near misses
- softer incidents such as computer abuse and attempted visits to banned websites.

In the IT security world, security tools or components themselves generate a host of information about:

- vulnerabilities detected

- servers patched

- intrusion attempts

- authentication errors

- attacks on firewalls and attacks that passed the firewalls

- attacks prevented by intrusion prevention systems (IPS)

- the number of password resets, user adds/deletions and access control list (ACL) changes

- virus outbreaks and time to resolution.

The key is to determine which metrics are useful for the organisation, the security strategy and the audience, discussed below.

SECURITY BALANCED SCORECARD

One technique to identify the metrics required is via the balanced scorecard. This is a business strategy that, in a nutshell, ensures that every action links back to stated corporate goals. If it can be shown that there are certain objectives within the security group that will directly help the organisation achieve its broader set of objectives, then there is a basis for making a business case to senior level management. The balanced scorecard looks at where the organisation is going, to see how the security group's work contributes to that, and then it links security priorities and service to those activities. The balanced scorecard has a typical structure based around four different perspectives (Volchkov 2013):

1. Financial performance – what contribution can security make to improve the financial performance of the organisation?

2. Operations and process – how can security improve organisational operations or processes?

3. Customer relations – how should security be perceived by its customers (internal and/or external)?

4. Culture, learning and growth – how can security maintain the desired organisational culture and its ability to evolve and improve?

This technique is a well-known management tool. It allows the security team to monitor its performance and helps position the security team as a partner of other parts of the business, making its contribution explicit. It also helps influence the senior management team to take ownership of security issues and security's added value as it ties directly to organisational objectives (Volchkov 2013).

It reflects that financial performance and operational measures alone do not convey all the information required to assess the contribution of different activities. The four perspectives – financial, operational, customer relationships and culture (or learning and growth) – should have links to objectives to be achieved, and then a limited number of metrics linked to those, e.g. three or four metrics (Volchkov 2013). Figure 7.1 shows an example of objectives and associated metrics.

Sphere	Objectives/ Initiatives	Metrics
Financial Performance	• Manage the cost of security • Complete projects on budget • Improve the efficiency of leak controls	• Security Total Cost of Ownership vs number of employees • Cost of security incident resolution • Percentage of emails covered by controls vs. number of employees • Number of data exfiltration incidents investigated
Operations & Process	• Reduce the risk of information leakage by negligence • Protect confidential information • Maintain system availability • Implement best practice	• Penetration tests conducted • Number of rule breach findings • Number of confidential information breaches or near misses • Availability statistics associated with security • Assessment of maturity
Customer Relationships	• Provide quality guidance and advice to customer/staff • Ensure customer /staff security awareness of policy • Prioritise projects that align to business goals	• Overall customer/staff satisfaction with security guidance and advice • Number of people completed awareness training • Number of significant projects that security rep on project board for vs total number of significant projects
Culture & Learning	• Build and develop security culture	• Result of security culture survey

Figure 7.1   Example of a security balanced
scorecard adapted from Volchkov (2013)

If there is a format of dashboard or scorecard being used in other parts of the business, try to adapt the security one to those. When identifying performance against metrics, do not ignore the starting point. Whenever a decision is made to undertake a significant project or programme, do whatever is possible to establish a baseline first. It is critical to have a baseline so that you know where your starting point is. As described in Chapter 4, a security culture assessment can provide this baseline for measuring improvement.

SECURITY MATURITY

A security maturity rating provides the organisation with information about its levels of preparation or its security status. Security maturity should be evaluated so that initiatives can be prioritised and aimed at addressing deficiencies (Volchkov 2013).

Formal maturity models consist of questionnaires based around standards or frameworks (for example ISO 27000, COBIT or NIST), or they may propose their own catalogue of measures (Volchkov 2013). They rate the maturity of processes against a scale, usually from 1 to 5.

For example, a rating of 1 might be where a process is in initial stage maturity; 2 is where a process is developing; 3 is where a process is defined; 4 is where a process is managed; and a rating of 5 means the process is optimised.

As mentioned, a maturity model is a useful tool for informing the business of its security status, and it helps explain security programme initiatives. Table 7.1 shows an example of a security risk management maturity model (PSR 2015).

Table 7.1   Example of a security risk management maturity model. Reproduced by permission, New Zealand Protective Security Requirements (PSR)

Assessed Maturity Rating		Description
5	Optimised	Security is a strategic issue for the organisation. Long-term planning is in place and integrated with business planning to predict and prepare for protective security challenges. Effective continuous process improvement is operating, supported by real-time, metrics-based performance data. Mechanisms are also in place to encourage, develop and test innovations.
4	Managed	Day-to-day activity adapts dynamically and automatically in response to situational changes. Quantitative performance measures are defined, baselined and applied to ensure security performance is analysed objectively and can be accurately predicted in advance.
3	Core	Policies, processes and standards are well defined and are actively and consistently followed across the organisation. ... Governance and management structures are in place. Risk assessment and management activities are regularly scheduled and completed. Historic performance information is periodically assessed and used to determine where improvements should be made.

2	Basic	The importance of security is recognised and key responsibilities are explicitly assigned. At least a base set of protective security measures are planned and tracked. Activities are more repeatable and results more consistent compared to the 'informal' level, at least within individual business units. Policies are probably well documented, but processes and procedures may not be. Security risks and requirements are occasionally reviewed. Corrective action is usually taken when problems are found.
1	Informal	Processes are usually ad-hoc and undocumented. Some base practices may be performed within the organisation, however there is a lack of consistent planning and tracking. Most improvement activity occurs in reaction to incidents rather than proactively. Where practice is good it reflects the expertise and effort of individuals rather than institutional knowledge. There may be some confidence security-related activities which are performed adequately, however this performance is variable and the loss of expert staff may significantly impact capability and practice.

SECURITY RISK MANAGEMENT

Risk management is the ultimate objective of all security activities and assurance efforts. A key goal of all types of corporate security is to reduce adverse impacts to acceptable levels. An effective security programme should therefore show a trend in impact reduction.

An indicator of effective risk management is an overall security strategy and programme for achieving an acceptable level of risk. This is done through the basic security risk management process:

1. understanding applicable threat assessments;

2. identifying critical organisational assets; those assets that are important for the ongoing operations of the business – the 'crown jewels' so to speak. Then an assessment of their Business Impact Level (BIL) should be made by assigning a value to assets based on the impact arising from the compromise of confidentiality, loss of integrity or unavailability of the assets.[1]

3. identifying relevant security risks to the organisation and those critical assets;

---

1   Standard definitions of BILs exist. A simple example can be found at New Zealand's Protective Security Requirements website, http://protectivesecurity.govt.nz/home/protective-security-governance-requirements/business-impact-levels; or more detailed BIL tables can be found at the UK's CESG website, www.cesg.gov.uk/publications/documents/is1_risk_assessment.pdf.

4.   assessing and evaluating the level of risk by identifying their impact and likelihood;

5.   the appropriate treatment and mitigation of risks; and

6.   monitoring and reviewing risks to ensure they remain at an acceptable level.

Once the factors that will have the biggest impact on critical assets and their risks are identified, it is then possible to deal with them to reduce risks to acceptable or tolerable levels. These can then be presented to senior management for signing off, that they are satisfied with the planned mitigations and the residual risk levels.

The key to security metrics is to show that any money spent is worthwhile – and where more expenditure would result in a saving. When it is possible to show measurable improvements in any aspect of security, the programme can be justified, and it is possible to obtain additional funding and support.

Techniques for Presenting Metrics to Senior Managers and Staff

The discussion of metrics above offered some guidance on the content required to present to senior management. We now look at how to present and convey that information succinctly in useful, interesting and engaging ways. The ways that I have found most successful for presenting metrics is either in the form of a dashboard (or scorecard) or in a programme status report.

DASHBOARDS AND SCORECARDS

Long reports are not a good format for senior managers who need concise information quickly in order to make decisions. They also take too long to prepare and do not focus on the pertinent information required. That is why dashboards and similar presentations tools were created.

A dashboard provides management with a snapshot of information without the need to spend a significant amount of time reading documents. It is similar to a car's speedometer or other dashboard instrument, displaying important information at a glance. The obvious benefit of a dashboard is that a few relevant factors are selected to be displayed and the audience can see the status of the factor at hand (Purtill 2012). By picking the right ones it is possible to fulfil the audience's information needs with the dashboard, and little else. The following outlines a few points to note about dashboards (Purtill 2012):

- They can be as simple as a PowerPoint presentation, or a little more sophisticated if done in a spreadsheet (e.g. Excel) or using software to create real-time information.

- Be realistic about graphics: four on a page is enough; add more pages if necessary. Every item on the dashboard must earn its keep and not overwhelm the user.

- Mix things up: don't use just bar graphs, or just line charts etc.

- Consider data security when developing and distributing a dashboard, to avoid security programme dashboard information getting into the wrong hands. Classify and label the dashboard appropriately if the information needs to be protected, or consider other methods of protection.

Provided here are two examples of a dashboard that could be used for monitoring security awareness and security culture programmes in organisations, to give an idea of the desired look and feel (Figure 7.2 and 7.3).

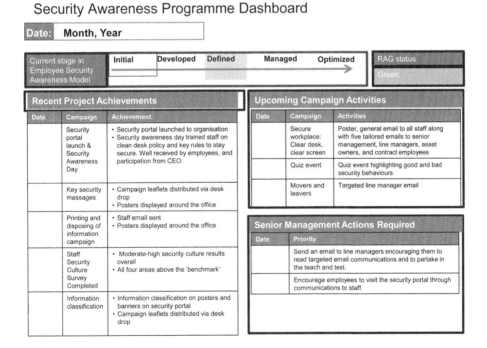

Figure 7.2   **Sample security awareness programme dashboard**

Security Culture Survey Dashboard

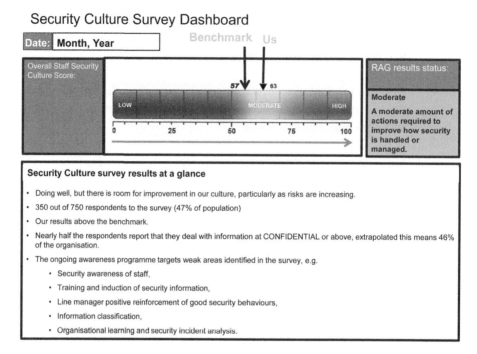

Figure 7.3   Sample security culture survey dashboard

PROGRAMME STATUS REPORTS

Programme status reports are another common way of presenting progress and present metrics to senior management. These convey more information than a dashboard or scorecard, and consequently are slightly longer. The main idea behind these reports is to track progress against objectives: if the tracking of objectives can be mapped to maturity, all the better for conveying 'where you are at' to senior management. Table 7.2 on pages 140–141 is an example of a programme status report that assigns a RAG status (red, amber, green) to objectives and a maturity scale.

How Often to Report

Progress reports should be provided at appropriate intervals: too often and it is possible to lose the audience's attention. Quarterly is recommended to allow enough time to clearly show the impacts of change. Reporting should not be more frequently than monthly.

Longer-Term Considerations to Maintain a Strong Security Culture Programme

DO NOT TAKE ONGOING SENIOR MANAGEMENT SUPPORT FOR GRANTED

Whilst senior management support is required at the outset of a work programme, their continued support should not be taken for granted, and so efforts should be made to maintain senior support in the longer term. Some members of senior management may waiver in their support at times during the programme depending on their different priorities or areas of focus.

A large amount of work is usually successfully done at the outset to gain senior management buy-in to the programme. However, some time later, when for example a new campaign or initiative is introduced, it may became apparent that some executives need to have their support solicited again and rekindled. It is particularly important to ensure that enough care is taken to ensure that the senior management understand the requirements for the programme and support it.

This can be overcome by creating special briefing messages that the senior level sponsor can deliver at senior meetings to solicit ongoing support. It is also important to convey a steady stream of new information or thought around security. Keeping the information fresh helps stimulate people's interest. Factoring in further senior management buy-in to the programme along the way can ensure continued support.

HOW DOES A PROGRAMME SURVIVE NOT HAVING A SIGNIFICANT SECURITY BREACH?

Lack of a significant security breach or issue can mean that the organisation does not readily see the value of good security practices, procedures and controls. Effective security practices, or the security department's ability to steer the organisation through potential issues, can mean that those issues become invisible to senior management. An impact of this can be that the organisation begins to reduce or withdraw its investment in security.

The security team need the senior management team to 'feel' the serious consequences of issues, but also to divert the organisation from actually experiencing them first hand.

Table 7.2 Security risk management programme status report

PROGRAMME STATUS REPORT

Period ending	
Submitted by	
Distribution	Executive Team

Security Programme Maturity

Assessed Maturity Rating		Description
5	Optimised	Security is a strategic issue for the organisation. Long-term planning is in place and integrated with business planning to predict and prepare for protective security challenges. Effective continuous process improvement is operating, supported by real-time, metrics-based performance data. Mechanisms are also in place to encourage, develop and test innovations.
4	Managed	Day-to-day activity adapts dynamically and automatically in response to situational changes. Quantitative performance measures are defined, baselined and applied to ensure security performance is analysed objectively and can be accurately predicted in advance.
3	Core	Policies, processes and standards are well defined and are actively and consistently followed across the organisation. Governance and management structures are in place. Risk assessment and management activities are regularly scheduled and completed. Historic performance information is periodically assessed and used to determine where improvements should be made.
2	Basic	The importance of security is recognised and key responsibilities are explicitly assigned. At least a base set of protective security measures are planned and tracked. Activities are more repeatable and results more consistent compared to the 'informal' level, at least within individual business units. Policies are probably well documented, but processes and procedures may not be. Security risks and requirements are occasionally reviewed. Corrective action is usually taken when problems are found.
1	Informal	Processes are usually ad-hoc and undocumented. Some base practices may be performed within the organisation, however there is a lack of consistent planning and tracking. Most improvement activity occurs in reaction to incidents rather than proactively. Where practice is good it reflects the expertise and effort of individuals rather than institutional knowledge. There may be some confidence security-related activities which are performed adequately, however this performance is variable and the loss of expert staff may significantly impact capability and practice.

Work stream	Key deliverables	Current maturity	Desired maturity	How measured	Comments and progress
Reporting a security issue	Employees know how to report a security issue and where to go for help	2	4	Measured through survey	
Security awareness training	New employees undergo security awareness training. Existing employees undergo a refresher	2	4	Measured through training records	

Table 7.2 *continued*

		Current risk		Residual risk	
Organisation-wide view of security risks	The organisation has a correct, current and compressive understanding of its security risks	2		4	Security risk register is developed for all areas of the organisation. Security risk register is reviewed quarterly.
New and emerging security threats	There is early warning in place for emerging threats	1		3	Measured through the corporate risk register. Measured through discussion of security risks at management meetings.
Security is embedded in project management	Zero high risks/errors resulting from security not being considered at the project level	1		3	All risk registers for significant business cases or projects are reviewed by the security team.
Security risk mitigation	Mitigation/action plans are put in place with agreed timeframes	2		5	Measured by all security risks on Corporate Risk Register having action plans by the next monthly reporting period. Effectiveness of action plans are tested by security team.
Major accomplishments since last report					
Major activities for the next month					
Key risks currently affecting the programme					
Description	Current risk	Mitigation	Residual risk		

The question arises, how does a security group survive when they avoid significant security breaches? One thought that remains is should all incidents be avoided, or should some perhaps be 'manufactured' in order to ensure the organisation learns lessons from its risky behaviour and stays the course of good security? One way to manufacture security breaches is to set up a 'safe' environment for them to occur in. For example, have an unknown person, but known and trusted by the security team, attempt to see how far they can get into the organisation. How far could they penetrate without proper security passes and authorisation and what information they could they find? This is a human factor penetration test of sorts. This would provide an opportunity for senior management to potentially 'feel' the discomfort of a security breach, without the devastating consequences.

Alternatively, as previously discussed, it is important to discuss at senior level any security breaches concerning other organisations reported in the news. That is, drawing attention to the fact that other organisations are suffering security breaches while your organisation is not. Link this to the security or security culture programme's success. Zero breaches are an inverse achievement metric. This is an example of when achieving a zero result is good. Contrast this with other enterprises in the sector to reinforce the value of the organisation's security efforts.

FLEXIBLE WORKFORCE PLANNING: RIGHT PEOPLE, RIGHT TIME, RIGHT SKILLS

It is rare that one person has all the skills required to see a programme through from inception to completion. Often the key is to recognise the need for different skills at different periods and to recruit accordingly. Whilst it can be difficult to engineer if not carefully planned, having the right person in the right place at the right time is crucial to organisational performance. The benefits of correct workforce planning include (Lambert 2009):

- cost reduction

- assurance that business plans can be delivered

- improved service quality

- improved staff recruitment, retention and engagement.

As an example of how to deliver flexible workplace planning, through a programme's lifecycle, it may be possible to employ different people to lead the security team at different times, with different, but accurate, skills for that period. For example, in the requirements definition stage a policy development specialist might be employed. When this person moves on or their contract ends, it would be wise to attract and employ a people and culture specialist to oversee the delivery and embedding of those policies. In short, there are different skill sets required at the different stages of implementation.

This sort of planning could be called a 'living workforce strategy': the output from a typical workforce review is a report which represents a static 'point in time' view of the organisation's workforce requirements (Lambert 2009). In contrast, there is value in creating a living workforce strategy – a shared view of the future business plans matched to the skills of the workforce, developed in collaboration between HR and the business. This strategy should be underpinned by data models, adaptable to different business scenarios, built through engagement of key business managers and turned into practical recommendations that will work 'on the ground' (Lambert 2009).

INVOLVE STAKEHOLDERS THROUGHOUT THE PROGRAMME

An engagement approach is a good way to ensure stakeholders are involved throughout the programme. Ensure they have defined and formal roles and responsibilities so that their purpose is clear. This can help achieve:

- alignment of expectations through each programme stage;

- improved information flow;

- incorporation of good practice and latest thought leadership in security, including access to academic research and development;

- validation of security programme approach and decisions made;

- assistance in building a business case for security requirements; and

- shared organisational risk with stakeholders.

This approach can be delivered through early engagement with stakeholders from the outset. The key is to identify and give stakeholders defined roles; for example, is there an appropriate stakeholder to conduct technical design reviews and advise the security team? Is it appropriate for other stakeholders to take on an audit function? This can be done through stakeholder mapping, either inside or outside the organisation. Then engage with the stakeholders and formally invite them to participate in security projects in appropriate roles, for example working groups or risk review panels.

Summary

What gets measured gets managed. The key is finding the right metrics that are useful for the management of the programme and to track performance. Presenting these to senior level leaders in an engaging and succinct manner will give security the attention required to justify spending and secure future investment.

The long-term success of a security culture programme also needs attention. Matters such as not taking ongoing senior management support for granted come into play, as does considering the impact on the commitment of management of *not* having a significant security breach. Run the programme with the right people, with the right skills at the right time or flexible workforce planning, and embed and engage key stakeholders throughout the programme.

The next chapter features case studies illustrating how organisations are applying security culture mechanisms. In particular, it highlights the development and implementation of a security culture and people risk management programme from the London 2012 Olympics.

References

Hubbard, Douglas W. 2010. *How to Measure Anything: Finding the Value of 'Intangibles' in Business*. Hoboken, NJ: Wiley.

Lambert, Paul. 2009. Tomorrow's workforce: Right people, right place, right skills? *HRZone*. May 19. Accessed May 25, 2015. http://www.hrzone.com/lead/strategy/tomorrows-workforce-right-people-right-place-right-skills.

Ponemon Institute. 2013. *Understanding the Economics of IT Risk and Reputation: Implications of the IBM Global Study on the Economic Impact of IT Risk*. White Paper. United States: IBM Corporation.

———— . 2014. *2014 Cost of a Data Breach Study*. Traverse City, MI: Ponemon Institute.

PSR. 2015. Protective Security Capability Model. *Protective Security Requirements NZ*. Accessed May 25, 2015. http://protectivesecurity.govt.nz/assets/Uploads/Protective-Security-Capability-Maturity-Model.pdf.

Purtill, John S. 2012. How to use a dashboard to improve management reporting. *Purtill & Company Ltd*. Accessed May 25, 2015. http://www.purtill.com/files/Purtill-Documents/Dashboard.pdf.

Volchkov, Andrej. 2013. How to measure security from a governance perspective. *ISACA Journal* 5, 44–51.

Chapter 8

Case Studies

The purpose of this chapter is to provide six case studies about:

- Designing and implementing a security culture programme for the London 2012 Olympic Games.

- Improving the security communications of a large company delivering vital services.

- A small start-up business designing in security from the very start.

- A government organisation maintaining compliance with government security policy frameworks.

- Risk management culture – developing a risk management culture of which security is a part.

- How staff action led to a privacy breach and how a small healthcare organisation handled it.

This chapter presents a number of case studies from organisations describing the assessment, design or implementation of a security culture programme using some of the tools and techniques described in this book. The varied types of organisations show how each programme can be applied differently to each unique setting and context.

The first study is from the Olympic Delivery Authority responsible for building the stage for the London 2012 Olympic and Paralympic Games. Several unique challenges were inherent in this project, including an immoveable deadline and high-risk threat profile. Following this we look at a large company responsible for providing vital services to the public who viewed proactive, rather than reactive, communication as key to the success of their security programme.

Next is a study of a small start-up business looking to instil a strong security culture from the outset. Here it was important to consider the business lifecycle so that a security mind-set would spread once more people joined and the business grew. The fourth case involves a government organisation which, in compliance with a government security framework, was required to demonstrate visible steps towards developing and maintaining a culture of security.

The next case study shows a broader view of security culture, called risk culture. It described how an organisation developed and implemented a risk aware culture, of which security was a part. The final case concerns an organisation which suffered a privacy breach due to the unwitting actions of an employee. This organisation had to learn the hard way, but improved its processes and security culture as a result of the incident.

Case Study 1:
Olympic Delivery Authority

Raising the security culture bar for the Olympic and Paralympic Games in London 2012

The Challenge

Changing an organisation's culture and undertaking organisation-wide initiatives is difficult under any normal circumstances, and attempts routinely fall short as they fail to alter behaviour. Add to that an immovable deadline, intense public interest and a stakeholder group that reaches far beyond the organisation's boundaries – to include numerous government departments, private organising committees, the Mayor of London and the prime minister – and you begin to get a feel for some of the pressure and expectations of preparing and hosting the London 2012 Olympics and Paralympics.

The Olympic Delivery Authority (ODA), a public body, was responsible for constructing the venues and infrastructure for London 2012, charged with building the stage for what the British Prime Minister David Cameron called 'the greatest show on earth'. The challenge was to get the building company, with its *Bob the Builder* mentality ('Can we fix it? Yes we can!'), to balance delivery pressures against raising the bar in terms of security culture for the new heightened threat environment fast approaching. A strong security culture in the ODA would mean that employees were security-aware. ODA staff needed to understand why security was important and be motivated to follow security policies, even when they were not being supervised.

As the Games drew nearer, the Olympic Park and its venues changed from construction sites to operational Games venues and an appropriate shift in gear was needed to ensure the safe and secure running of the Games. It was well known that the London 2012 Games would have a threat profile like no other Games before it. No United States-based Olympics had faced as many threats as London's, from Irish splinter groups to lone-wolf suicide bombers, said terrorism experts such as David Tubbs, a former FBI official who helped coordinate security for the Salt Lake City and Athens Games (Watson 2012), so security was paramount. Jonathan Evans, head of Britain's MI5 intelligence agency, warned that the Games presented an attractive target.

On top of this, these changes had to be implemented within the ODA's complex organisational and workforce structure: a small number of directly employed staff; a large, diverse, multisite delivery partner; and numerous subcontractors. This unique make-up comprised people with varying degrees of interaction with information and understanding of information security; including IT experts, administrators, personal data handlers in the Olympic Park pass offices and construction workers. To complicate the picture further, the ODA had only been created in 2006 and would cease to exist in 2014, thereby requiring its workforce to be laid off at the appropriate time and business to be wound down in a cohesive way.

There were only 12 months to undertake a culture change programme to improve staff security behaviours and awareness. The organisation, its staff, contractors and third parties had to move through various organisational phases: Olympic Park construction/big build; test events and overlay; full operational readiness in time for the Games; exit strategy.

Background

As a public body, the ODA needed to report centrally on government security standards, including its procedures for handling personal data, data breaches and its ability to meet protective security standards. Further to this, compliance along the supply chain was required and had to be negotiated with other Olympic partner organisations. Therefore, the ODA held and exchanged significant amounts of sensitive information with multiple partners and third parties via email, paper and by word of mouth. It was essential to protect this information from compromise, not only for legal reasons but also to protect the ODA's reputation and for the security of London 2012.

The ODA's security culture change programme was managed by its Information Security team, whose remit was to provide assurance and confidence that data could be shared safely and securely, reducing unnecessary risk to personnel, infrastructure, reputation and cost. The ultimate goal of the team and the programme was to protect the ODA, its information and data from being used for the purposes of terrorism, espionage, media attack, organised crime (e-crime, theft and fraud) and commercial malpractice. A major information security breach could seriously disrupt the exchange of information for the ODA and its supply chain, which could have a serious knock-on effect on construction programme delivery and the reputation of the Games. The information security cultural change programme supported the ODA's objectives through delivering the following programme elements:

- the development of a risk alert culture to prevent avoidable breaches that could lead to damaging incidents;

- reporting of security incidents and suspicions;

- encouraging others to behave securely;

- preparing ODA employees and suppliers for the potential increased risk of targeted criminal activity and media focus in the lead-up to the games;

- understanding the importance of security to the ODA and delivery of the games;

- understanding that all employees/suppliers are responsible for their actions;

- achieving compliance with mandatory government and legal requirements (e.g. data protection);

- adopting correct security techniques.

In meeting these goals the organisation had to take an appropriate and proportionate approach to enable it and its supply chain to share information and not be unduly constrained.

As expected, levels of security progressed over time. In the beginning there was a low security threshold as the organisation was new; but it grew and developed from requirements definition through to a rationalisation and tightening of approach, through to eventual close-out in line with the ODA's activities and milestones.

Whilst technology plays a fundamental role in protecting information, people's behaviour is often at the root of data security breaches. The ODA recognised this and invested in a cultural change programme to establish the expected behaviours of employees and third-party suppliers. The ODA recognised that enhancing staff behaviour and educating on key responsibilities could be the most effective measures for an overall enhanced information security posture.

Theoretical Basis

The programme was based on the following theoretical principles of security culture, organisational culture and behaviour change espoused by the UK's Centre for the Protection of National Infrastructure (CPNI):

- Security culture is *essential to an effective security regime* – it is important for organisations to think about it in relation to their strategy and practices to foster an effective security culture.

- Organisations are typically *proactive about physical and IT security*, but *not in relation to how people behave*. The best security procedures may be in place, but what is critical for upholding security is how people interpret or comply with them.

- It is important to *create a culture* within the organisation where employees are *security-conscious* and thinking about *how to protect* information, people and services.

- Any programme should measure *underlying attitudes* towards security in the workplace – what *enables* and what *gets in the way* of good security – in order to effect change.

- It is important to look at the *mechanisms* that drive positive behaviours to determine if they are *aligned with the culture* of the organisation.

- It should also look at how *consistent* behaviour is across the organisation, how *compliant* people are, or where there might be *risks*: e.g. *a major breach, loss of information, loss of intellectual property (IP) or damage to reputation.*

How the Programme was Delivered

From 2009 to 2011, the ODA commissioned various short security awareness activities. In 2010, the ODA commissioned the CPNI to perform a security culture audit using the latter's 'SeCuRE' (Security Culture Survey) tool methodology. This report identified that generally the ODA was doing well with regard to its security status, but there were areas for improvement, including:

- security competence of staff;

- praise and recognition for good security behaviours;

- line manager contact and communication around security issues;

- security emphasis to combat complacency; and

- classification so that the value/level of information and how it should be protected was done more consistently.

In response to these areas for improvement that SeCuRE identified, in 2011 the ODA went out to mini-tender for a consultancy to design and implement an integrated end-to-end programme for the remaining 12 months to the Games.

The culture change programme had to be in sync with other organisational stages, meaning a heightened state of security culture could not be reached sooner than required. If the programme missed these milestones or if timing was poor, the programme risked being rejected altogether. A staged approach over 12 months was instrumental to the programme's smooth and successful integration into the organisation. This was based on an in-depth understanding of the ODA's environment, stakeholder groups, target audiences, senior management objectives and high-risk areas. Integration into the business occurred as follows.

STAGE 1: CURRENT STATE ASSESSMENT

The basis for smooth integration was an understanding of the current environment. The current employee and third-party perception of behaviour towards information security was determined and the current security culture identified through surveys and interviews. High-risk areas based on previous audit reports were identified, and a strategy to address these risks was defined, along with a set of baseline measures to gauge the success of the programme and the return on investment.

STAGE 2: TARGET STATE AGREEMENT AND TOP-LEVEL COMMITMENT

It was vital for the successful integration of the programme into the business to obtain buy-in from senior stakeholders to sponsor the programme; to provide support within their division; and to remind them of the importance to act as role models to their employees.

Stakeholder buy-in and sponsorship was obtained through workshops, interviews and a presentation to the Executive Management Board, with previous lobbying of key influencers and decision makers. The cultural change strategy was agreed with senior stakeholders, along with the communications plan, project plan and key performance indicators (KPIs).

STAGE 3: NORMAL DELIVERY

Having defined both strategy and target audience, the programme was launched by focusing on raising awareness of its existence and purpose before tackling the deeper issues of information security responsibilities and expected behaviours.

An engaging launch informed employees and third parties of the programme; promoted information security as a vital part of London 2012; and instilled the message that their actions have a direct impact (both positive and negative) on the security and success of the Games.

Strict brand guidelines were applied to all communications and brand-approved images ensured that information security messages were identified as an integral part of the ODA's business. The key slogans, all relevant to the ODA's business objectives, were:

- Do your bit to help leave a lasting legacy after the Games.

- Be secure until the finish line.

- Security is a team sport.

STAGE 4: GAMES READINESS

Through regular awareness campaigns focused on key themes, such as Clear Desk Policy and Information Classification, the culture change programme educated employees and third parties to adopt the desired techniques and behaviours; report security incidents and suspicions; and encourage their colleagues to behave securely. This was measured through the aforementioned KPIs.

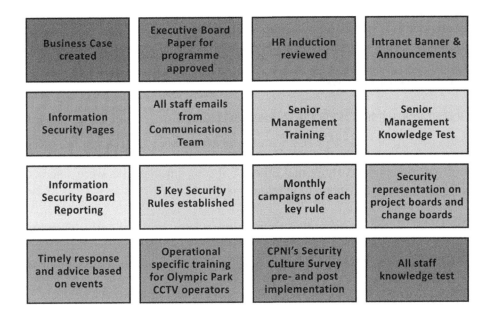

**Figure 8.1   Olympic Delivery Authority security
culture programme components**

The programme comprised a number of elements which were embedded in the fabric of the organisation (Figure 8.1). Each department, group and individual was encouraged by the CEO to play their part by treating security as a 'team sport' to ensure they were 'secure until the finish line'.

To create this mindset, it was important to provide training and to build awareness of security and the growing need to protect the successful delivery of the Games. Vulnerabilities could come from anywhere in the organisation – from uncollected documents in printers and over-the-shoulder laptop 'eavesdropping', to discussing London 2012 business on social networking sites and unsupervised visitors roaming office premises or the Olympic Park. The message was that everyone could do their bit to increase security, but that security needed to be as unobtrusive and consistent as possible to be successful.

Key Programme Outcomes

Feedback on the comprehensiveness of the holistic corporate security programme and its implementation was made by Ernst & Young in its 2012 Audit report in relation to meeting the UK Government mandatory security requirements, of which information security is one of several key elements. Feedback from the CPNI on the ODA's SeCuRE results highlighted that the results were consistently above the UK national average. The main project outcomes were as follows:

OUTCOME 1: IMPROVED DATA PROTECTION

There was greater protection of ODA information due to more rigorous security controls implemented at optimal times. It also meant that risks were assessed and pragmatic organisational decisions made.

The ODA shifted its security culture from a less regulated 'private sector' style to a typically more cautious and regulated 'public sector' style. This progression allowed a building of security to match the threat environment. This was delivered by:

- creating security policies and standards that were aligned with the government security frameworks;

- delivering government standard ICT accreditation, a formal process whereby information security risks are identified, assessed and mitigated in an IT system, which enabled the organisation to focus on vulnerabilities and risk management;

- involving Information Security representatives on organisation-wide project boards and changing boards to influence at an early stage;

- conducting the CPNI's SeCuRE security culture survey before and after programme implementation to measure progress. This enabled the ODA to further justify its business case for security awareness and culture change with the executive board. It focused the programme on areas for improvement as well as highlighting strengths. This gave voice to staff opinions on security and how it could be improved.

- employing the right people at the right time depending on the organisation's lifecycle stage. The ODA employed a policy maker when defining governance and mobilising the IT function. It then embedded the policy and security culture through employing a chartered organisational psychologist, and a communications and people specialist to lead the Information Security team and manage the awareness programme.

- A security awareness and communications strategy for a 12-month period was created to allow incremental culture change to be planned. This took into account the organisational environment and business activities.

OUTCOME 2: THE PROJECT INFLUENCED BEHAVIOUR AT ALL LEVELS OF THE ORGANISATION

Subject matter experts were used to design the programme, and bespoke communication methods were used to get messages across. In selecting an individual to spearhead the effort and a consultancy to work with, the importance of 'influencing security behaviours at every level of the organisation' was acknowledged. Communication skills and behaviour change techniques topped the list of CV and tender prerequisites, along with information security knowledge/experience. This was delivered through the following:

- The project lead and consultancy were judged against their expertise in communications strategy, psychology and behaviour change, as well as their understanding of government security strategy and commercial information security practices.

- Monthly project performance reports were presented to the Information Security Board and the Executive Management Board by the programme's senior champion, using engaging dashboards. Importantly, the dashboard specifically highlighted areas of action for the senior team, so that they knew what was required of them.

- A bespoke 'Information Security Zone' was created which made policy information easily understandable and accessible.

Measurement and Benefits of the Programme

The ODA's security culture and awareness programme was measured throughout in order to be adapted to ensure it delivered results in the most effective and efficient manner. A baseline was defined to measure the programme's success and return on investment. The approach was to enhance the ODA's security culture in stages: by taking employees and third parties from being unaware of their information security responsibilities to being aware of them, to committing to the ODA's security principles and demonstrating the desired behaviours.

Significant achievements included the transition of staff behaviour from unaware to aware of their information security responsibilities within five months of the programme's launch and prominent senior management endorsement throughout, as a result of thorough research, planning and measurement. Of particular importance was endorsement by Dennis Hone, Chief Executive at the ODA. His visible support of the programme helped instil the key security messages and demonstrate the programme's importance to the business.

The KPIs were based on areas where improvements were sought by the ODA in order to improve its security culture. These were grouped into behavioural and technical KPIs as shown below.

BEHAVIOURAL QUANTITATIVE KPIS

- Fewer losses of laptops, BlackBerrys and information.

- Reduced issues identified in desk sweep exercises.

- Positive feedback from employees.

- Increased contact with the Information Security team.

- Increased contact with the IT helpdesk.

- Increased reporting of incidents.

TECHNICAL QUANTITATIVE KPIS

- The CPNI's SeCuRE tool to gather staff views on security within the ODA.

- Dedicated role-based intranet site ('Information Security Zone') KPIs include:

  - page hits (including number of unique users)

  - top 20 search terms

  - site feedback

  - page ratings provided by users

  - Interactive learning and examination module KPIs include percentage of successfully completed tests.

After successfully completing phase one of the ongoing awareness programme, a defined KPI framework for future measurement and development was established. The sustainable approach that was adopted for culture change meant that the ODA was dedicated to measuring, improving and re-evaluating all elements of the programme to ensure its success. The evolving threat landscape and movement of employees around the business made this an integral element of the project.

Summary

The ODA achieved great success, and built a strong reputation. The information security cultural change programme further strengthened this reputation by highlighting to the board the importance of appropriate information security behaviours at all staff levels and making it an integral part of the ODA's core business of preparing, delivering and building a lasting legacy for London 2012. Specifically, in relation to legacy, the ODA designed its awareness materials so they could be shared with its parent department, the Department for Culture, Media and Sport (DCMS) and the Olympic Park Legacy Company (OPLC), now the London Legacy Development Corporation.

The programme allowed employees and third parties to see security as a support mechanism rather than a barrier to business activities. One of the straplines featured on communications was 'Security is a team sport'. This encapsulated the essence of the programme and helped endorse secure behaviours and perceptions of security, which positively improved the security culture of the ODA.

Senior management visibility increased within the organisation as a result of endorsing the programme as an important internal initiative vital for delivering the Games and the London 2012 legacy. Senior management actively participated in activities during the Security Awareness Day, demonstrating their commitment to information security. Chief Executive Dennis Hone, in particular, played an integral role and continued to visibly endorse and support the programme.

The Information Security Zone functioned as a central point of contact for information. This was linked to via the ODA's intranet site and provided useful information on information security around the office environment and in employees personal lives, For example, employees could find out how to protect themselves against credit card fraud and how to secure their home computer.

The communications strategy that was implemented actively complemented and supported the existing ODA culture, ensuring its seamless integration into the business. Throughout the programme, a strong combination of communication materials encouraged employees and third parties to contact the Information Security team to discuss any security concerns or report any incidents. The security team's visibility and approachability ensured that they and all employees were integral to the protection of ODA information and the integrity of the London 2012 Olympic and Paralympic Games in the run to the finish line.

A Large Company Supplying Vital Services

Engaging staff in security through improving communication

The Challenge

This large company needed to provide its vital services in the safest and most reliable way possible. Any interruption to services due to a security breach was not just unacceptable, but also potentially life threatening. However, the organisation and its staff did not generally think about security in their day-to-day work, unless something went wrong.

Background

In the past, the organisation had not strategically considered their security culture. Any communication with staff about security was reactive: that is, only following a security incident might staff be informed in order to avoid a reoccurrence. There was no proactive and planned communication about security. There was also no measurement of the organisation's security culture, so any security activities carried out did not have a baseline measurement and there was no real sense of what had been successful or not.

How the Programme was Delivered

The organisation decided that the best place to start was to measure its security culture to establish the gap between their current culture and their aspirational one. While surveying staff, additional organisation-specific questions were added to make the survey more relevant to staff. They also worked closely with the communications team to ensure that the correct branding and messages were imparted, as well as the reasons why a security survey was being conducted at that time. Through working with HR, they were also able to time the survey in and around other organisational surveys and initiatives to ensure a good response rate and avoid overburdening staff.

Key Programme Outcomes

The survey highlighted some specific areas for improvement, which were aligned to the desired security culture – in particular a need for more staff information and training to improve their security understanding and behaviour. The organisation also needed to find ways to communicate with staff better, and more often, about security so that it would be more at the front of their minds. It was important that staff knew how to report security issues and understood any changes to the company's threat profile, so that they could help protect the organisation, its staff and its vital services. To help in these areas, the security culture programme consisted of the following:

- Reviewing and refreshing security policy and procedures. This required engaging with and getting input from different parts of the business, which was a positive activity in itself. There was a particular focus on getting the security breach reporting procedure right.

- Making the intranet's security pages more user focused and, therefore, easier for staff to navigate to find information needed. The use of key personas – line managers, personal assistants and field staff – to identify target audiences and their requirements helped in designing the website.

- Working with the communications team on the most effective ways to issue new security procedures and policy. Brief security messages were created for screensavers and posters based on the different personas in an effort to make messages more relevant to individual staff. They also found out how the changes affected staff and used the points of view of existing members of staff in the communications to reinforce messages using peer influence.

- Refreshed security messages in staff inductions. Clear and engaging messages in new staff inductions helped ensure they were brought on with the right messaging. Through working with the privacy team, messages were also identified for inclusion in the induction package which built favour with the legal team and improved efficiency.

- Developed security balanced scorecard. Performance metrics for the security department were linked to business objectives and strategy to better reflect how improved security behaviours add value for the organisation. It also helped show security as company-wide activity and not just the remit of the security department.

Measurement and Benefits of the Programme

Through measuring the security culture programme via the balanced scorecard the company was able to determine the impact of the interventions mentioned above. In addition, based on the security team's successful interactions with the business, they were invited to monthly management and team briefings where they could deliver new security messages to ensure it remained a priority and also uncover obstacles to good security within the business. There was also buy-in to repeat the security culture survey on an annual basis as a benchmark and to monitor the progress of the security culture.

Summary

While the security culture survey revealed several areas for improvement, the decision to focus on security communication, information and training helped the company make some good first steps towards its aspirational security culture. It would have been too large a change if it had decided to improve everything identified in the survey. Instead, incremental change was possible through putting in place good foundations (e.g. fit for purpose policy, procedure and security intranet pages), and the company secured early quick wins which found favour with different areas of the business.

A Small Start-Up

Designing in security from the very start

The Challenge

As a small start-up company with big plans to grow, this organisation wished to create a security culture from the outset. It would be handling sensitive customer data and had proprietary intellectual property to protect. Scalability was also a consideration. The company initially had just a handful of employees, and any security culture interventions would need to be sensible and pragmatic for a small business. However, there were plans for the organisation to triple in size over the coming year as operations ramped up.

Background

The owners set up the business following a particular process framework methodology, so the task of developing a security culture was also carried out in line with this methodology, as shown in Figure 8.2.

The middle box of Figure 8.2 identifies the task and it subcomponents. The task was to develop and embed a security culture in the currently small number of employees. The aim was to then spread this culture to newly recruited staff once the company began to grow. Therefore, the security culture programme needed to be scalable and fit for purpose.

As can be seen in Figure 8.2, following the process framework, in order to complete the task the pre-conditions required were time with senior staff and/or shareholders who understood the company's vision and could participate in a workshop to consider the current security culture and the aspirational culture required to fulfil that vision. At this workshop they would answer questions such as: 'What security behaviours does the

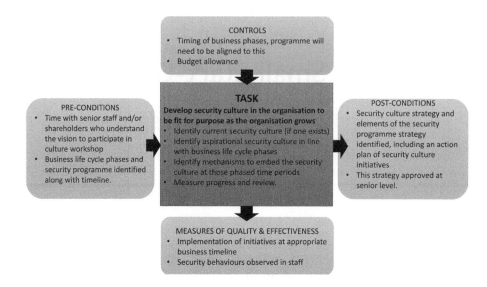

Figure 8.2 Process framework used by a small start-up for developing a security culture

organisation want staff to have?' and 'Would the security behaviours for the small start-up company stay the same once the organisation started to grow?' The second pre-condition required was to understand the business development cycle and how the security programme would fit into this.

The post-conditions to exist after the task was completed were the development of a security culture strategy along with elements of the security programme being further identified. This would include an action plan for security initiatives against the phases of business development. The last post-condition was that the strategy be approved and committed to by senior management.

The controls to consider were the timeline of the business development phases. The development of the security culture strategy needed to be completed prior to, for example, the recruitment of new staff. It was also important to consider any budget constraints.

The measures of quality and effectiveness for the task were the implementation of security initiatives at appropriate times as the organisation grew and the observation of staff exhibiting the desired security behaviours.

How the Programme was Delivered

Culture scoping meetings were set up with key stakeholders, such as the Director of Operations, to discuss the benefits of a security culture programme and approve the process described above relating to required pre- and post-conditions, controls and measures.

It was decided to conduct a workshop with the start-up employees and appropriate shareholders to ascertain the company's required security culture and security behaviours. The business lifecycle was a key consideration as it was expected that the overall security programme itself would progress, tighten up and rationalise over time. This meant that security culture initiatives would change and develop over time as well.

Initially, the organisation had a low security threshold as it was a new company and was limited in its application of best practice. It was initially non-compliant with security standards and frameworks.

The second stage in its business cycle was defining requirements. Once the organisation's security programme requirements were defined, security and/or information assurance roles could be established – for example, security officer, security manager, senior risk owner. It was at this stage that the business case and strategy for the security programme was approved, including requirements for its IT network protection, and technical solutions identified.

The third phase was a delivery stage, when information assets were defined and classified according to requirements of confidentiality, integrity and availability. Protective marking classifications were also implemented. During the delivery phase the organisation needed to raise security awareness in order to influence staff behaviour, and processes were enhanced so that they were fit for purpose. The organisation carried out risk assessments to ensure it understood its current threat profile.

The final stage of security programme growth related to further integration, embedding, testing and assurance activities. With governance, risk management and security operations activities set up, the company moved on to the maintenance of its security culture programme, assurance activities and security incident management. The mechanisms required to fulfil this business development vision were mapped to this timeline (see Table 8.1).

Key Programme Outcomes

The security culture strategy and action plan, including initiatives, were delivered in an 'appropriate and proportionate' way so that the organisation and its supply chain were able to share information and were not unnecessarily constrained.

Table 8.1   Map of security culture initiatives against the business development stage

Business development stage	Examples of initiatives planned and implemented
1. Low security threshold	These were implemented by the small team immediately and consisted of what is sometimes called 'basic good housekeeping':
	Discouraging the posting of information on social media until the launch of the company at stage 3, delivery.
	Locking laptops and papers away at the end of the day or when not in use.
	Shredding confidential information generated.
	Using strong passwords and changing them regularly.
	Encrypted USB sticks used while information in transit.
	Peer support used to influence and monitor behaviour.
2. Requirements definition	At this stage, more formal security initiatives could be introduced, for example:
	Security roles were identified for staff.
	Security responsibilities were included in job descriptions, contracts with suppliers and performance objectives.
	A system of information classification was defined and launched.
	Loose talk about confidential company information in public places was discouraged.
3. Delivery	In the delivery stage, formal security initiatives were positively reinforced and disciplinary procedures carried out for lapses. Ongoing security communications were developed to help staff understand the key security messages.

4. Integration, embedding, testing and assurance	Ongoing security communications programme implemented.
	Security balanced scorecard reported quarterly performance.
	Spot checks and assurance visits checked compliance against security policy.
	Peer support and coaching encouraged to support continued high standards of security behaviours.

Measurement and Benefits of the Programme

The security culture programme ramped up as the business itself grew and became more mature. A few basic good housekeeping behaviours developed into formal policy which was communicated and reinforced through formal procedures and peer support.

The benefit of this approach was that by starting the company with positive security behaviours it was easy to formalise these and staff did not feel like they were having anything taken away from them or being stopped from doing things they had previously been allowed to do. For example, if staff are initially not encouraged to lock away laptops and papers and then a new policy is brought in which decrees they must do so or face punishment, it can feel like the security group is being difficult and behaviour change is more difficult to achieve.

Summary

As the organisation continues to grow, a very real security mindset is in place which continues to develop momentum and is spread from employee to employee. The security culture strategy is reviewed at least annually and grows with the company and its staff. Security has become 'the way we do things around here'. Staff regulate each other's security behaviour, and near misses are usually caught before developing into a breach.

Case Study 4:
A Government Organisation
Maintaining compliance with government security framework

The Challenge

Building a strong security culture makes good business sense, but a government organisation must meet additional statutory and legal requirements concerning data protection, freedom of information, public records and intellectual property. There are also often requirements of compliance with security policy frameworks, often including security culture as an important part. Government organisations then are required to have a plan for creating the right culture, take visible steps to support and participate in that plan, and have plans to monitor progress and compliance. In this instance, for this case study, a security culture programme was non-negotiable. The benefit of this is that an agenda for security culture existed; however, often senior management buy-in is still required for the programme to be truly successful.

Background

Work had already been done to identify the type of culture the organisation needed, and a cultural statement drafted which documented and formalised this approach. The focus was then on identifying which mechanisms needed to be improved within the organisation and which were operating efficiently, to develop the aspirational culture.

All staff were required to complete a security culture survey so that the different areas of the organisation could be compared. Although the areas differed, they were all working towards one shared vision, so some basic standards and security behaviours were expected. The survey would provide a benchmark for security culture performance.

Staff were informed about the survey via a link to an article on the intranet's weekly newsletter, through senior management meetings and in the CEO's quarterly update meeting with all personnel. The chance to win a prize was also offered as an incentive for completing the survey. Workshops and one-to-one interviews were also carried out with staff, alongside the survey.

A statistically viable sample size was worked out using readily available online survey sample size tools, and a dedicated confidential mailbox was set up for responses.

How the Programme was Delivered

The importance of senior management buy-in was not taken for granted and so the high-level results of the survey were first briefed at this level. This helped secure support for the interventions which would follow based on the results. The results indicated areas the organisation was performing well in. For example, it empowered people with security responsibilities and the security incident reporting procedure was clear.

There were also a number of areas that needed improving and these became the focus of the security culture programme. Specifically, positive reinforcement for good security behaviour was weak; training on security threats could be improved, along with more time being spent on security at induction and the inclusion of security in performance appraisals. There was also a requirement for better change management through planning and communications, and more could be done to ensure the organisation learnt from its past security mistakes. The results were then communicated to the rest of the organisation and the plan of action to improve them publicised on the intranet.

Key Programme Outcomes

The security culture programme designed around the above results consisted of refining the organisation's key security messages down to roughly five to seven important issues that staff should know. These simplified security messages were agreed by the senior management team, and the entire programme was based around promoting these over the course of the year as per a communications plan. One of the key messages concerned a clear desk policy: that staff clear paperwork off desks and lock laptops and/or computer screens if not in use and when not at their workstation. Regular office checks were carried out and compliance was rewarded by a chocolate left on every clear desk.

A review of the security awareness induction package was also carried out. One of the most effective mechanisms was found to be peer pressure. In areas of the business where individuals reminded colleagues about correct security policy, the correct behaviours soon followed. Therefore this message was encouraged via the security culture programme. This played to the psychological phenomenon that, if people are given permission to 'help' and 'coach' their colleagues they feel more comfortable correcting their behaviour and are more likely to give them a friendly reminder.

Measurement and Benefits of the Programme

One of the benefits of the survey was that it jump-started the organisation into thinking about security. The communication of the results to staff and the subsequent security programme initiatives all helped maintain the momentum. The security culture survey would therefore be completed on an annual basis to measure progress and refresh staff's memory.

Results of the security culture programme itself were reported at senior management level. Some of the metrics of success used were the results of security compliance inspections; security breaches per month; and the number of functional area management meetings attended by a security representative.

The senior management team also approved the appointment of security champions in the different areas of the business to promote local issues. This position was given sufficient status to make it attractive to staff and to give security itself the status it deserves.

Summary

This organisation initially developed its security culture programme in response to government security policy requirements. However, the success achieved with a basic programme has meant that further initiatives, such as the establishment of security champions, have been approved to further embed security culture in the fabric of the business.

Case Study 5:
Risk Management Culture

Developing a risk management culture
of which security is a part

The Challenge

This organisation wished to build more than just a security culture; it wanted to instil in its staff a risk management mindset. Security was important, but in this organisation it made sense to fit security risks into a bigger risk-aware culture. The aspiration was for risk culture and management to be embedded in strategic planning, capital allocation and other processes in daily decision making and thinking. The organisation wanted an early warning system in place to notify the board and management of risks above established thresholds and/or tolerance.

For this to become a reality the organisation needed to move from risk management in silos to a consistent organisation-wide approach. Staff needed to believe in risk management, effectively developing a culture of which security risks would be a part.

Background

The organisation was not necessarily new to risk management. In fact, there were already excellent examples of risk management and culture; however, the approach to risk management was not consistent throughout the organisation and not all risks were managed through the same process and in the same way. This made it difficult for the organisation to compare like-for-like risks across the business. A high risk in one department was measured against a different yardstick to a high risk in another department.

The vision was to have a one-stop shop for risk management, for risk management be part of every business activity, irrespective of business area and type of risk – be it safety, security, financial, reputation and so on.

Some communication with the business had already begun around risk management and a risk policy and draft framework had been started. Some staff had even attended external training sessions on risk management. Workshops with different areas of the business had identified some risks to be included on the corporate organisation-wide risk register; and high and extreme risks on that register were reported monthly to the board. But there was still no real momentum or take across the business for risk management. A clear strategy was needed to be driven and implemented.

How the Programme was Delivered

The organisation's vision for risk management was clear: simply stated, it was for risk management to be part of everything done and every decision made, no matter what type of risk or where it originated. This clear vision allowed an approach and strategy to be developed.

The approach and direction was presented at the executive level and then at board level for approval. It was understood that for the programme to be successful it would require the heads of department to support it. Once senior level support was achieved, the programme was delivered through a number of initiatives explained below.

The foundation for risk management in the organisation came from the risk management policy. This was refreshed to incorporate the consistent organisation-wide strategy for risk management agreed at executive level, and roles and responsibilities were clarified.

The risk evaluation framework was also refreshed. In particular, the word pictures for risk severity were updated with language that made sense and would relate to the different business units. For example, the severity of a cyber incident for the operational arm was expressed as the stoppage of operations or systems being compromised, whereas the severity of a cyber incident for the commercial arm was expressed as the difficulty or inability to secure future contracts and win tenders due to damaged reputation. The risk evaluation framework would be the main tool for risk assessment, so a lot of time was spent making it as fit for purpose as possible, and it was constantly challenged and tested. It was attractively designed to fit on one page, and laminated copies were regularly given out in discussions on business risks.

Existing risk management processes and procedures were identified across the organisation, and the departments responsible for them worked alongside risk management staff to ensure the approved risk evaluation framework was used. This required the risk management team to work with the project management office, operational and engineering areas of the business, the safety department, shared services and the commercial teams.

An in-house risk management training course was created to suit the specific needs and context of the organisation. The course covered not only pertinent theoretical principles of risk management, but also (and more importantly) how staff should apply risk management practically in their day-to-day jobs, including opportunities to do so during the sessions.

A risk review panel was set up, whose role was to qualify, moderate and challenge submitted risks before they were accepted for the corporate risk register. The panel consisted of senior subject matter experts (SMEs) from across the main areas of the business. There was a quorum of permanent panel members, and appropriate guests were invited to discuss relevant risks from their knowledge and experience when required: for example, a human resources SME would be invited when a people risk was presented to the panel, or a legal representative brought in when a legal view on a risk was needed. A security SME was a permanent member of the review panel to help ensure that security impacts were consistently represented across the organisation.

Software improvements were made to the organisation's risk database which enabled employees to self-sufficiently submit risks. Automated dashboard reporting of risks from the database was also developed to reduce reliance on the risk management team to provide risk reports. This helped the business to own risk management in their areas of work. Risk management was also integrated or better aligned with change management processes, which again ensured consistent use of the risk evaluation framework.

An ongoing communications and education programme was developed to run alongside the changes mentioned above. The risk management pages on the intranet were refreshed according to user needs, making it easy for staff to find what they needed in relation to risk management or further help.

Key Performance Outcomes

The programme increased transparency through a standardised methodology and risk management system across the business. Local risk registers were identified and input into the organisation-wide corporate risk register. The number of qualified risks in the database grew, which gave a better view of risk across the business. If not knowing your risks is like standing in a dark room, then this organisation had really turned the lights on, effectively arming the business with knowledge to make sound decisions.

The programme of work along with the communications and education programme meant that the risk team were increasingly invited to join business risk discussions. This was a positive sign of the programme's success.

Measurement and Benefits of the Programme

A number of metrics were used to assess the effectiveness of the programme, and a project status report template common to the organisation was used to report progress quarterly to the executive team.

Metrics were aligned to programme objectives and the Risk Management Standard (ISO 31000:2009), specifically Clause 3 ('Principles of Effective Risk Management') and Annex A, which outlines the 'attributes of effective risk management'. This provided a basis to evaluate the extent to which the organisation was conforming to the standard. A maturity scale was also used to demonstrate how performance to programme objectives mapped to risk management maturity. For example, if a programme objective was 'staff know how to raise a risk and where to go for help' then it was mapped to risk management maturity as it progressed from a maturity rating of two out of five, whereas more mature objectives such as 'the business has an accurate and organisation-wide view of risk' was mapped to four out of five on the maturity scale. Each programme objective was mapped accordingly to show the risk posture of the organisation.

One of the aims of the risk programme was to 'spread the word' about risk management. The organisation wanted employees to talk about what risk management was, its benefits, how to do it and who was involved. The training course designed and delivered in-house was the major vehicle for this, along with word of mouth – an impressive 140 people from different areas of the business were trained in six months. As more people received training, so more people began talking about risk management; more people came to speak with the risk management team; and more questions about whether important decisions had been risk assessed were asked.

Summary

The organisation is now a year into its risk culture programme and although not yet complete, the success and momentum of the programme has been impressive – so much so that one of the organisation's clients asked it to deliver a risk management training course for them.

Learning the Hard Way

How an employee's actions led to a privacy breach and what this small healthcare organisation did about it

The Challenge

A data or privacy breach in the healthcare industry is a big deal, as material held is both protected health data and personal identity information. Reports such as the *Experian 2014 Data Breach Forecast* state that this industry is picked to be a hotbed of increasing data breaches and thefts (Experian Information Solutions 2013). The healthcare industry is more vulnerable due to its large network of providers and its increasingly interconnected nature. From local GPs to large hospital networks, its sheer size and multiple data handling points provide a much larger target for cyber criminals and increase the opportunity for misuse or mishandling of data. It is also not generally as well protected as other industries with sensitive data such as the finance industry.

However, data breaches and thefts do not have to be complicated or conducted by cyber criminals to be damaging. This case study concerns an unsophisticated privacy breach in a small Healthcare Provider. It was caused by an unwitting employee who was unaware that what they had done was wrong in any way.

Background

The owner of the Healthcare Provider received a letter from its administrative employee notifying them of their intention to reduce their number of shifts as they were planning to move to a new business venture in an unrelated field. Once the new business was up and running the administrator then intended to leave altogether.

The next week the owner received another letter from the employee, this time a sales letter that introduced the owner and the new business, stating: 'You might know me as the administrative person at the Healthcare Provider ... .' That morning a number of patient complaints were made to the Provider, who had also received this blanket sales letter.

When the employee was questioned they said that they had sourced the information from the electoral roll, and not from the Provider's patient database. However, because the employee aligned themselves with the Provider by way of introduction, whether or not the information was from the database, the damage had been done. The complaints were that patients had not authorised the Provider to share their contact details in this way. In the patients' minds, if their contact details were being shared illegally, what other information was also being mishandled?

How the Programme was Delivered

The Provider had to manage three factors: 1) the human resource issue; 2) security protection, security awareness and security culture gaps; and 3) any damage to its reputation and brand.

The first factor was a human resources issue and had the potential to escalate into a grievance if the proper process was not followed, so an employment lawyer was used to navigate this. Understandably, disciplinary meetings were held and formal processes followed to deal with the staff member who, for a number of weeks after the incident, still did not believe they had done anything wrong.

To deal with the second factor, gaps in security protection/awareness/culture, an assessment was undertaken by the Provider. It decided to review its management of personal data through the information lifecycle. It made sense to address how data theft could occur by people both outside the organisation and by employees inside the organisation. The main gaps identified were a lack of IT infrastructure security and a lack of security awareness and security culture among staff. The data breach itself happened due to an employee's silly mistake – they should have known better; but the Provider, as their employer, should have played a bigger part in ensuring that they did know better. As part of the privacy and security review the Provider looked at:

- processes for gathering, handling, storing and disposing of electronic and paper data;

- the protection of its information technology systems, such as intrusion prevention and detection systems, firewalls and audit trails;

- the role and level of security of individuals with access to personnel and client information;

- how to communicate with clients and the public about its policies and what the response plan is in the event of a breach.

Based on the findings of the review, the Healthcare Provider improved its security programme through the initiatives outlined below.

The patient database was already secured using password protection and firewalls. However, as a result of the review the Provider realised they did not have a good strategy in place to monitor and protect the organisation from cyber threats to all inbound internet traffic; nor did they have security measures to monitor and protect all outbound internet traffic against data leakage loss and theft. Given the increasing risk to the healthcare industry, the current risk exposure and the Provider's weak security status, this was something they felt they could not ignore.

In order to really 'wrap their arms around' the sensitive data they held, the Provider decided to carry out some penetration testing and also to engage an internet perimeter protection service at the gateway between their business and the internet. Just as the patients trusted their healthcare to the Provider, so the Provider decided that a Managed Services Solution Provider (MSSP) for its IT security would be far superior to anything the organisation could achieve on its own.

Access to systems was limited to those with a 'need to know'. Access was also blocked to idle computers through automatic locks or screensavers that required a password from an authorised user. Where possible they also avoided using communal computers and generic or group log-on and passwords. Passwords were also changed so that employees were required to use a combination of upper- and lower-case letters, numbers and symbols; and a policy put in place to ensure passwords were changed regularly.

To address security awareness and security culture, the organisation put its employees through personal data handling and information security refresher courses to reinforce its key policy messages about data collection, use, disclosure, security, storage and disposal. Key messages were:

- Patient information should only be used for the purposes for which the information is collected.

- Log-on to computers using alphanumeric passwords, and change them regularly.

- Don't ask for customers' personal data in front of others, and ensure they have privacy when entering PINs.

- Check signatures and verify that customers are who they say they are.

- If there has been tampering with terminals or databases, inform management.

- Keep customer information under lock and key.

- Shred all confidential waste, including payment card information and photocopies of ID documents.

- Clean desk tops every night.

- Only access databases when authorised.

- Lock systems when not in use.

(Credit Institute of Canada 2008)

The Provider reserved the right to check the audit function of firewalls, encryption programs and password schemes, with the assistance of the MSSP to check logging data and audit trails for unusual or suspicious activity, e.g. employees accessing data not relevant to daily business transactions (Consumer Measures Committee 2011).

They also took the opportunity to refresh information disclosure procedures so that all staff were clear about how and when information could be disclosed, particularly to a third party.

With regard to the third factor – damage to reputation and brand – apologies and explanations were made to those individual clients who made complaints. While only obliged by legislation to reveal privacy practices when requested, the Provider chose to send every patient a simple one-page letter describing its privacy policy, information security practices and the steps taken to protect patient data, including the provision of an MSSP for internet perimeter defence. This communication with its customers was to help mend any damage to the Provider's reputation and brand.

Key Performance Outcomes

As a result of the actions taken, the best result for the Provider was that it was able to retain all its patients. The staff also reported greater clarity and confidence in their information security responsibilities. Staff training has also become part of the mandatory induction process to avoid this sort of breach in the future.

Measurement and Benefits of the Programme

The Provider reasoned that the cost of an MSSP was far less than the cost of a cyber-attack or employing its own full-time staff to manage IT security. It also increased the Provider's compliance and level of assurance, and improved business continuity. There was also the added benefit of being able to assure patients of the protection afforded their sensitive information.

The training for staff on handling personal data and information security practices was well received as it gave them a base level of knowledge. After the training staff felt comfortable about challenging or questioning others if they thought policy was not being followed. It also created a coaching atmosphere as staff felt empowered to support and help each other keep the patient information protected.

Summary

While the Provider learnt the hard way about the impact of a data breach, it provided the burning platform required to review and upgrade its standards in relation to information security. It has also set itself apart from its competitors with its fit-for-purpose, effective and affordable protection from online threats and data leakage, loss or theft. This situation gave the Provider the opportunity to be proactive in relation to data breaches to prevent them from happening in the first place. However, in the event of a reoccurrence, the Provider and its staff are well prepared to deal with it to minimise any damage.

References

Consumer Measures Committee (CMC). 2011. *Identity Theft Kit for Business: Tips for Reducing the Risk*, June 8. Accessed May 26, 2015. http://cmcweb.ca/eic/site/cmc-cmc.nsf/eng/fe00092.html.

Credit Institute of Canada (CIC). 2008. Identity theft: Practical tips for credit professionals. *To Your Credit: CIC e-newsletter*, Spring. Accessed May 26, 2015. http://www.creditedu.org/Resources/newsletters/newsletter_spring_08/collections.cfm.

Experian Information Solutions. 2013. *Experian 2014 Data Breach Forecast*. http://www.experian.com/data-breach/data-breach-industry-forecast.html [registration required for access].

Watson, Traci. 2012. London Olympics, where security isn't a game. *USA Today*, December 7. Accessed May 26, 2015. http://usatoday30.usatoday.com/sports/olympics/london/story/2012-06-27/london-olympic-security-is-no-game/56151246/1.

Appendix A:

Example Proposal for Funding for a Consultancy to Deliver a Security Programme Business Case

PROPOSAL FOR FUNDING

DELIVERY OF AN INFORMATION SECURITY, SECURITY CULTURE and PEOPLE RISK MANAGEMENT BUSINESS CASE

Table of Contents

1. Project Objectives and Output

This piece of work is to develop the business case for implementing a security culture that will reduce security risk from people in the organisation. The business case will be used to get approval and funding for [Organisation X's] Information Security and Security Culture Programme.

The development of the business cases will enable [Organisation X] to approve funding in order to:

- mitigate identified information security, security culture and people risk threats and risks;

- meet its corporate responsibilities and comply with government standards;

- manage and control information security, security culture and people risk through a single, coherent programme-funding structure.

The outcome will be the business case for presentation and approval by the [senior executive team/accountable officer/security risk owner].

The proposed business case will examine the requirements, outcomes and benefits; define and evaluate options for meeting the requirements; and recommend the best value for money.

2. Business Need

The primary objectives for the Security Programme are:

1. To drive the programme based on assessments of threats, vulnerabilities and risks.

2. To protect:

    a) [Organisation X's] current and future critical information assets and any information assets [Organisation X] holds on behalf of others;

    b) [Organisation X's] information network infrastructure.

3. To direct and operate the programme to agreed standards, whether they be information security, security culture or people risk.

4. To test [Organisation X's] security processes and procedures against threats.

5. To minimise and respond appropriately to security incidents.

There are a number of key drivers for the security programme:

- [Organisation X's] corporate responsibility and compliance with government standards.

- The threats, vulnerabilities and risks from assurance reports and audits and assessments in the organisation's risk register. [If these do not exist it may be a good idea to develop them.]

- The need to protect critical information assets [these may appear in an organisational asset register; if you do not have one, again another useful thing for the organisation to develop] and IT infrastructure.

- Costs and value for money of options delivering the mitigation of assessed threats, security strategy and the required level of security standards compliance.

A number of security activities have already been initiated within [Organisation X] for which business cases are required, and these activities need to be coordinated effectively and appropriately funded. The main activities are:

- X [sample activities might be external audits and assessments; a review of governance and management arrangements for security; the development of a security strategy; development of an information asset register and security awareness activities]

- Y [sample activities might be technology projects that have been initiated to upgrade network access controls; manage remote and mobile usage; oversee web usage and content; monitor events and incidents]

- Z [list anything else you currently have in place]

An outcome of the proposal is to devise a coherent structure and approach to these initiatives and to evaluate and recommend the best value for money in delivering the requirements of the programme.

3. Business Case Structure

The business case structure is proposed as .... [a diagram may be included here].

- Strategic case: needs benefits, scope, requirements and risks

- Economic case: options and evaluation

- Commercial case: procurement strategy and approach

- Financial case: funding requirements and cash flows, including whole-life costs for projects and operations

- Project management case: project plans, schedules and controls.

4. Resource

It is proposed that [insert name and organisation] will deliver this project. [insert name] has the required experience and track record in developing security business cases and liaising with stakeholders. They have a strong background in [xxxx].

5. Activities Required

The overall approach to this assignment will be to:

a) Collate and analyse findings on information security, security culture and people risk to date. Draw on work and information completed and call on the knowledge and experience of those involved to date.

b) Identify gaps. Analyses can be completed and judgements made on these inputs.

c) Conduct exercises to fill gaps.

d) Evaluate all findings. Any gaps in what is required can be filled by reference to stakeholders and those involved in the projects; any specific additional pieces of work will be identified and agreed before proceeding.

e) Put together business case using findings.

Given an initial review of work and documentation to date, the activities involved in delivering the assignment are:

A. ASSIGNMENT SET-UP

a)   Gather and review all documentation currently available related to [Organisation X].

b)   Prepare and agree statements of scope, issues and potential options for the constituent parts of the business case for lead sponsor(s).

c)   Finalise and agree a template for the information security overview/ security culture and people risk business case and constituent business cases based on current organisational guidance, existing templates and current practice.

d)   Prepare gap analysis of information required for business case and arrange for that work to be completed. It seems likely that additional work will be required on finalising and assessing the scale of the requirements, and costing of delivery options. It is assumed that this work will be carried out and the outputs provided by others engaged in the programme.

e)   Prepare stakeholder list and engagement plan for review of issues and options, and agreement of the information security business case.

f)   Review plan in the light of work to date and gap analysis, and review progress with sponsor.

B. STAKEHOLDER ENGAGEMENT AND OPTIONS EVALUATION

a)   Meet stakeholders to discuss scope, issues and options.

b)   Revise scope, issues and options statement and agree with lead sponsor(s).

c)   Complete and write up options analysis for each case and review with lead sponsor(s).

C. DRAFTING AND REVIEWING BUSINESS CASES

a)   Gather all information and resolve issues relating to business cases.

b)   Draft information security/security culture and people risk business cases for review with main stakeholders.

c)   Meet stakeholders to discuss business case drafts.

d)   Revise, finalise business cases.

D. BUSINESS CASE APPROVAL AND CLOSE

a)   Distribute and present business cases for approach, including presentation material.

b)   Finalise approvals, file documentation and handovers.

6. Project Timeline

The project timeline expected, assuming work commencing [insert date].

a)   Assignment set-up: completed by [insert date]

b)   Stakeholder engagement and options evaluation: completed by [insert date]

c)   Drafting and reviewing business cases: completed by [insert date]

d)   Business cases approval and close: completed by [insert date]

7. Costs

[This will usually be stated in number of consulting days and day rate for each phase of work.]

Appendix B:

Example of Senior Executive Team/Board Meeting Paper

Agenda item: Security Awareness

Subject: Information Security, Security Culture, People Risk Programme

Recommendations

The Senior Executive Team is asked to:

- **Note** the attached paper detailing the Security Awareness Programme which is designed to maximise investment already made in information security at [Organisation X] and to increase organisational awareness of security across [Organisation], its suppliers and other delivery partners.

- **Promote** the Security Awareness Programme within your own areas by encouraging staff to engage with the programme and giving the programme a slot at team meetings.

- **Engage** with the programme – while the work of the programme will be completed by the Security team, it is important that the programme works with Internal Communications, Legal, HR, Information Management and IT teams in order to deliver messages in line with existing policies, processes and initiatives and business objectives.

Summary

This paper lays out the case for investing in a security awareness programme. The programme will increase compliance, improve control, reduce risks, reduce losses through security breaches and cut net costs by informing and motivating staff and creating a strong security culture.

Information is a fundamental asset to [Organisation X]. Security, that is confidentiality, integrity and availability of that information, is critically important to us. We hold and exchange significant amounts of sensitive information with multiple delivery partners and third parties via email, paper and by word of mouth. It is essential to protect this information from compromise – for legal reasons and to protect [Organisation X's] reputation.

[Organisation X] has already made investments in security, technology and information security. For example antivirus software and firewalls protect our information. But whilst technology is vital to protect information, people's behaviour is often at the root of security breaches.

Accidental or deliberate actions or inactions by our people pose a significant risk to our business. For example, people occasionally forget to change passwords on a regular basis or, worse, make the mistake of sharing passwords. They might email sensitive information to the wrong person or let visitors roam around the office unescorted. They might give out sensitive information over the phone or lose corporate laptops with sensitive information on them. These are everyday occurrences, not merely hypothetical examples.

Recent [audit reports/risk reviews/employee surveys/culture surveys/ security breach reports] have identified the lack of information security awareness and security culture in the organisation as an area of concern. This could undermine investment already made in security.

In addition, recent media focus on privacy and confidentiality breaches has intensified interest and potential reputational damage in this area. In addition, a weak security culture could mean an increase in more targeted criminal activity and cyber threat. A few of our employees, and outsiders in general, could try to deliberately defraud us, steal our information and intellectual property or cause havoc through denial of service or other cyber attacks. In [Organisation X's] daily operational activities, we are sharing more of our data with more third parties. It is important that we do not become complaisant as the organisation and people become busier.

Educating employees about being security aware with [Organisation X's] information and systems, and the reasons for why we have tightened controls on PCs and mobiles, will help us avoid potentially damaging data loss.

Now we need to invest into the underrated but vital human side of security. The Security Awareness Programme aims to:

- create a security-aware culture where people understand that information security is essential for [Organisation X] and how their actions directly impact the reputation of [Organisation X] and its ability to do business;

- raise employee and supplier awareness on the importance of handling information securely, their responsibilities, correct behaviours and who to contact with questions;

- provide help and guidance to employees and suppliers. They will not be turned into security experts, but will understand how to make a difference within their role;

- discharge the key remaining concerns of data handling review/risk review/audit findings.

Compared to further investment in security technology, the proposed awareness programme is a highly cost-effective means of improving information security that will derive more value from previous security investments.

KEY RISKS AND ISSUES

- Reputational impact on [Organisation X] due to security breaches and media coverage.

- Information security and safety risk to [Organisation X] and its people due to leakage and misuse of sensitive information.

- Degradation of security due to the misuse of [Organisation X's] information systems.

- Criminal activity and cyber threat to [Organisation X].

1. Background

[Organisation X] has built its security capability and implemented systems and processes to ensure successful delivery of its operations. Recent public and media focus on privacy and confidentiality breaches means that a single data loss incident can not only ruin the reputation we have built over the years but also put the business at serious risk. As [Organisation X] grows, more information is shared and people become busier and increasingly mobile; thus the likelihood of an accidental data breach increases.

A recent [audit/report/survey] highlighted that our employees were unsure of what constitutes personal and financial data; do not understand its value and the risks posed through poor handling; and are unaware of simple techniques to safeguard that information. Therefore, we must act now to educate our workforce and develop a culture alert to the risks to prevent an avoidable breach that could lead to a damaging incident.

2. Rationale

Cases of accidental data leakage and targeted online crime continue to grow exponentially. Information leakage incidents receive high media coverage and jeopardise the reputation of organisations, and potentially employees or customers if personal data is involved. Recent high-profile information leakage incidents include, for example [insert relevant data leaks here according to location, e.g. WikiLeaks, government privacy breaches, Sony, LinkedIn, Facebook].

[Organisation X] has been developing its security governance structure and has also been going through a system-hardening process to mitigate security risks and vulnerabilities to our network; but while policy and technology are vital, people's behaviour is still at the root of data breaches and information security incidents. A lack of a strong security culture in the organisation has been highlighted as medium risk to [Organisation X], which, unless mitigated, means the risk levels will increase. Enhancing technical controls will not resolve these issues. Our most effective and efficient way of addressing the risks is employee education and raising staff's understanding of how their actions or inaction can have a direct impact on the security of [Organisation X].

3. Programme Objectives

Our aim is to support the business to successfully deliver its mission, ensuring that avoidable security incidents do not disrupt our ability to deliver, or damage the long-term reputation of [Organisation X]. Our aim is not to make every employee a security expert, but to develop a culture that is alert to information security risks, where people understand the potential consequences of their actions and know who to turn to for further guidance or incident reporting.

Our aim is to engage with our staff and suppliers in a way that helps them understand:

- the value of information;

- the policies and controls in place to protect this information;

- the impact of a security incident (e.g. when certain information gets into the wrong hands);

- how their own actions or inaction directly affect the organisation;

- the key behaviours for safeguarding data.

We will use established awareness communication methods that have been proven effective, such as the following: [insert or delete as appropriate]

- Information security policies and standards will formally clarify the organisation's security rules for employees, managers, contractors and suppliers.

- Relevant laws, regulations and best practice standards (e.g. data protection/privacy legislation, industry regulations and ISO/IEC 27001) will be referenced and integrated.

- Straightforward plain-English guidelines and procedures will advise employees on how to comply with the corporate policies, standards and laws in practice.

- Background information on fundamental security concepts and issues, including newsletters, posters and screensavers, will be used to promote the information security brand.

- News of significant incidents will be included where appropriate. We may seek permission to circulate information from audit reports of other internal security assessments, as well as referencing major stories on information security from general news media. These are important as people commonly discount or underestimate the impact and frequency of incidents.

- Information security pages on the intranet – a central repository to answer all information security questions.

- Training and testing staff awareness through eLearning as a means of instructing our staff on the important subject of compliance, then confirming their understanding and awareness of the topic. All data is recorded in the learning management system and management information can be used to check the status of information security in the organisation.

- Concise and relevant messages tailored to individual target audiences, e.g. information asset owners or handlers of personal data.

- Bringing information security alive through the use of engaging stories with personal relevance.

- Technical details on specific information security threats or briefings on emerging threats will help incorporate appropriate controls into IT systems.

- Information security technical, cultural and awareness level metrics will be amalgamated into a dashboard for the organisation to review monthly.

4. Programme

The Security Awareness Programme will be delivered in X phases over the next X months. The programme will be overseen by [firstname lastname], Organisation X's [insert appropriate title].

To ensure the programme is delivered sensitively and appropriately for our people we will work with teams – such as internal communications, legal, HR, information security, third-party representatives, information management and IT – in order to ensure that we are communicating relevant, timely and effective materials that support our people to do their jobs.

PHASE 1: CURRENT STATE ASSESSMENT

- Understand the current security culture, current employee and supplier perception and behaviours towards security and high-risk areas.

- Establish a baseline to measure return on investment.

Output:

- Security Awareness Strategy

- Security Awareness Communication Plan

- Project Plan

- Information Security Dashboard – key performance indicators (KPIs) to measure the success of the programme and to be able to tailor it to effectively and efficiently achieve its objectives.

PHASE 2: TARGET STATE AGREEMENT/STAKEHOLDER ENGAGEMENT

- Gain stakeholder buy-in and sponsorship for the programme.

- Agree a strategy, communications plan and project plan.

Output:

- Agreed security awareness strategy, communication plan, project plan and dashboard KPIs.

- Senior management and head of department presentations.

- Identification and assignment of relevant key stakeholders to collaborate throughout the programme, such as internal communications, HR, IT and target audience representatives.

PHASE 3: AWARENESS PROGRAMME DELIVERY STAGE I – LAUNCH OF PROGRAMME

- Make staff and suppliers aware of the programme.

- Make staff and suppliers understand that information security is vital for [Organisation X]; that their actions have a direct impact (positive as well as negative); and that they know where to go for information (the InfoSec intranet portal as central repository).

Output:

- Information Security pages on the intranet as the central knowledge repository

- eLearning training (computer-based training)

Additional Awareness Communication Materials, [TBD], examples include:

- Senior management/stakeholder endorsement for awareness programme.

- Divisional line management cascade packs (including team briefings, team exercises).

- Security Awareness Day.

- Creation of key risk merchandise/collateral (e.g., posters, calendars, encrypted USBs, desk-drops, coasters, web banners) to underpin the programme.

- Share your experience of ID theft: employees volunteer their stories and receive tips on how to avoid becoming a victim.

- News stories and [Organisation X's] comment on them, including how to avoid similar things happening to us.

- Poll question of the week, to generate debate on news stories.

- Lunch and learns.

- Animations and films to attract attention to the programme.

- Use of a blog or discussion forum to encourage dialogue on topical issues.

- Overnight Clear-Desk Clear-Screen Sweep

- Measure KPIs to identify programme success, return on investment and to tailor the programme to improve its effectiveness and efficiency.

PHASE 4: AWARENESS PROGRAMME DELIVERY STAGE II – EMBED LEARNING

- Ensure employees and suppliers have adopted correct techniques and behaviours.

- Encourage employees, delivery partners and third parties to behave securely.

- Encourage employees and suppliers to report security incidents and suspicions.

Output:

- Information Security Portal (central intranet knowledge repository).

- eLearning training (computer-based training).

- Virtual Tour (a virtual office walk-through that highlights common information security risks in our daily working day).

- Additional awareness communication materials that have been proven effective will continue to be used to provide diversification and keep audiences engaged.

- Targeted relevant refresher messages to high-risk groups.

- Measure KPIs to identify programme success, return on investment and to tailor the programme to improve its effectiveness and efficiency.

5. Timeline

Month/year	Publish Security Awareness Strategy, including key performance indicators to measure the success of the programme
Month/year	Communicate top-down endorsement and the importance of the programme for the success of [Organisation X]
Month/year	Launch Information Security intranet pages and communicate key messages in order to address high-risk areas and raise awareness for the right behaviours
Month/year	Ongoing communications in order to further raise awareness and get staff committed to safeguard and securely handle information

Paper submitted by: [insert name]

Endorsed by (Executive Team Member): [insert name]

Appendix C:
Sample Security Communications Plan

MONTH	Briefings	Posters	Desk drop	General staff email	Tailored staff email
JANUARY	Executive Management Team				
FEBRUARY	**General staff:** Provide points for HR or communication team for CEO presentation. **General staff:** CEO to brief staff on upcoming security culture and awareness campaign during quarterly all-staff meeting	**General staff:** Poster: overview of 5 key security rules	**General staff:** Leaflet explaining 5 key security rules	**General staff:** Weekly all-staff email: article raising awareness of the Security Intranet pages launch	**Line managers:** Joiners, movers and leavers email highlighting the line manager's responsibilities for when staff join the organisation, move positions or leave the organisation
MARCH		**General staff:** Poster (placed in kitchen): addressing the importance of managing information securely **General staff:** Poster (placed by printers): addressing the importance of printing and disposing of information securely	**General staff:** Leaflet explaining the organisation's information classifications	**General staff:** Email highlighting responsibilities with regard to the printing and disposing of information	**Line managers:** Reissue the joiners, movers and leavers email highlighting the line manager's responsibilities as part of the mover/leaver process **Senior mgmt/line managers/business risk owners:** printing and disposing **Personal assistants (PAs):** printing and disposing; support to team **Personal data handlers (HR, legal, accounts):** printing and disposing, plus handling personal data

Induction	Organisational magazine	Functional area (FA) meetings	Intranet homepage banner	Security Internet Portal (or pages)	Other
oiners: oiners, movers and eavers induction – owerPoint slides ncorporated into he induction rocess to ighlight security equirements of taff and suppliers when joining the rganisation	**General staff:** Article explaining the importance of being aware of suspicious activity and how to report it	**FAs:** Briefing raising the awareness of the 5 key security rules			
		General staff: Briefing with a representative from the security team to discuss information classification	**General staff:** Launch of the Security Portal **General staff:** On information classification, directing users to the Security Portal	**General staff:** Summary statement to sit above animation on the Security Portal **General staff:** Animation: classifying information + banner on the Security Portal	**General staff:** Security Awareness Day – event to raise awareness of the Security Portal launch and Security Culture Programme

MONTH	Briefings	Posters	Desk drop	General staff email	Tailored staff email
APRIL		**General staff:** Poster addressing loose talk and social engineering **General staff:** Poster advertising the 'Spot the Risks' competition		**General staff: weekly email** Article raising awareness of the 'Spot the Risks' competition	
MAY		**General staff:** Poster: addressing password management			
JUNE		**General staff:** Addressing clear desk, clear screen policies **General staff:** Poster addressing ID passes and tailgating	**General staff:** Spot check card to be left on the desk of any employees 'failing' a spot check		
JULY		**General staff:** Poster – how to securely handle and store information		**General staff:** Email highlighting responsibilities with regard to data handling and storage	**Senior management** **Business risk owners** **PAs** **Line managers** **Personal data handlers** (e.g. HR, Legal, Accounts team)
AUGUST		Poster: 5 key security rules	Leaflet explaining 5 key security rules		

Induction	Organisational magazine	Functional area (FA) meetings	Intranet homepage banner	Security Internet Portal (or pages)	Other
		FAs: Briefing raising awareness of loose talk, social engineering and employee safety	**General staff:** On loose talk, directing users to the Security Portal	**Line managers:** e-learning module: to gauge awareness of responsibilities as part of the mover/leaver process Summary statement to sit above the animation on the Security Portal Animation: Need-to-know + banner on the Security Portal	**General staff:** 'Spot the Risks' competition: Easter-themed printout of an office-based scenario where staff are asked to identify security risks
			On password management, directing users to the Security Portal	Article on the Security Portal addressing choosing strong passwords, password sharing etc.) + banner on Security Portal	
			Asking 'Did you fall foul of the spot check' and directing users to the Security Portal	Article on keeping the workplace secure + a banner on the Security Portal Animation: tailgating	
			On managing information, directing users to the Security Portal	Summary statement to sit above the animation on the Security Portal Animation: mobile devices banner on the Security Portal	
				e-learning module: to gauge employees' awareness of their responsibilities; questions will concentrate on the 5 key security rules	

Index

For Product Safety Concerns and Information please contact our EU
representative GPSR@taylorandfrancis.com Taylor & Francis Verlag GmbH,
Kaufingerstraße 24, 80331 München, Germany

Printed and bound by CPI Group (UK) Ltd, Croydon, CR0 4YY
01/05/2025
01858368-0004